ANCIENT
GREEK
MYTHOLOGY

ANCIENT
GREEK
MYTHOLOGY

IAIN THOMSON

CHARTWELL
BOOKS, INC.

This edition first published in 1996 by the
Promotional Reprint Company Ltd,
Kiln House,
210 New Kings Road,
London SW6 4NZ.

Design and Layout © Promotional Reprint Company Ltd 1996

CHARTWELL BOOKS. INC.
A division of BOOK SALES, INC
P.O. Box 7100
Edison, New Jersey 08818-7100

ISBN 0 7858 0767 5

Printed and bound in China

HALF TITLE PAGE:

*Baalbek in Lebanon got its name from the worship of the
Phoenician sun-god Baal. The Greeks called it
Heliopolis. Captured in 332BC by Alexander the Great, it
fell to the Ptolemaic dynasty on his death. Today it is
famous for its Corinthian temples of Jupiter and
Bacchus (seen here) built in Roman times.*
Life-File/Stuart Norgrove

TITLE PAGE:

The Rape of Gannymede after Sir Peter Paul Reubens.
Christie's Images

CONTENTS PAGE:

*Ephesus is an old city; legend has it founded by
Androclus, son of Kodrus king of Athens. Renowned in
the ancient world for its shrine to the Anatolian mother-
goddess Cybele who melded with the Greek Artemis, it
remained ungarrisoned and unfortified until Alexander's
general Lysimachus moved the city to its current site.
The capital of Asia in Roman times, Ephesus depended
on its harbour and wqhen that silted up, the city died.
This picture shows the Street of Curetes which leads from
the Agora.*
Life-File/Andrew Ward

CONTENTS

Introduction

BELOW: The classic view of Greece: the Parthenon on the Acropolis in the centre of ancient Athens. The Acropolis was originally a royal palace until the 11th century; temples were built on it from about 700BC and the Parthenon we see today was built by the architect and sculptor Pheidas following Pericles's plan to rebuild Athens after its destruction in 480BC by the Persians. The building was started in 447 and completed by 438; the Propylea or entrance was built in 437-432 and the temple of Athena Nike (Victory) in 421. The Parthenon was dedicated to Athena — patroness of Athens. After nearly 2,000 years the Acropolis was devastated during wars between the Venetians and the Turks in the 17th century which saw the temple of Athena Nike destroyed and the Parthenon — which was used as an arsenal — lose its roof to an explosion. Almost as scandalous to some was the removal in 1801 by Lord Elgin of the Parthenon's frieze — the famous Elgin Marbles which currently reside in the British Museum.
Life-File/O. Svyatoslavsky

IN Greek mythology there were many stories about the family life of their gods and how the present dynasty of gods came to prominence and power. They also had myths about the creation of the world, but most of Greek mythology concerns the lives and loves of their heroes. The cult of heroes was widespread in ancient Greece and had its beginnings in the late 8th century BC when the Homeric poems became generally known. Local personalities then became identified with the legendary figures who had fought in the Theban and Trojan wars of the Heroic age: Heracles, Perseus and Theseus were among the most famous. Sometimes rites were performed at the tombs of prominent historical persons as heroes were believed to help the living in return for sacrifices.

For the Greeks there was no distinction between heroic mythology and ancient history — they were one and the same thing. These myths formed part of the ideology of the society — notions based more on tradition than fact. They constructed family trees which detailed all the human personalities of the myths. Although there are monsters in Greek mythology most of the stories are concerned with very human strengths and weaknesses. They are all about homicide, exiles, quarrels, seductions and illegitimate births.

It is difficult to pinpoint a time when the mythology arose. The *Iliad* and the *Odyssey*, both attributed to Homer, are the oldest surviving works of Greek literature but many of the stories in these books relate to traditional stories coming out of Asia Minor from about 800BC onwards. The mythological material contained in Homer was adapted and tailored to suit the tastes of the contemporary Greek society. The Greek myths of creation bear a strong resemblance to the stories prevalent in the Near East during the second millennium. Texts survive from about 1200BC from the Hittite culture in Asia Minor whose resemblance to the Greek myths are certainly close. Various theories have been put forward as to how and when direct or indirect borrowing might have taken place, but there can be little doubt that versions of earlier and eastern stories were known to the tellers of the Greek creation myths and influenced them.

Wherever they originated, the Greek myths still have a power and vivacity today which belies their age. They have been an inspiration to artists and writers throughout history, and continue to hold their fascination today.

Classical Greece

Greek culture and civilisation started in the late second millennium BC with the rise to power of Mycenae. The great epic of Horner hearken back to his time – but by the end of the 12th century BC its civilisation was in ruins. Greece rose again between 900 and 700BC and, in competition with the Phoenicians and Carthaginians, began to colonise the Mediterranean. The growth of the city states – particularly Athens, Sparta and Thebes – the defeat of their Persian enemies and the spread of their culture through their colonies reached its brilliant apogee under Alexander the Great. Following his death the Hellenistic Age would end only when upstart Rome took over.

Who Were the Ancient Greeks?

THE rise of classical civilisation in Europe can be traced back to the wanderings of a few barbarian tribes late in the second millennium BC. As early as 2000BC the first tribes began to move down into the Greek peninsula from the north. The earliest to arrive were the Acheans; they were soon followed by the Ionians and the Aeolians. These tribes, each speaking a different dialect of the Greek language, settled amongst the people already living on the peninsula (these earlier inhabitants had come from Asia Minor, probably c3000 BC). From the indigenous population these newcomers learned how to build cities, they also borrowed some elements of their language and started to worship some of their gods. From this developed the great age of Mycenae, whose rulers and their battles are part of Greek mythology — Agamemnon, Menaleus, Clytemnestra and the Trojan War.

With the arrival of the barbaric Dorians from the north around 1100BC, Greece was plunged into a dark age in which society fell apart and the skill of literacy was lost. These newcomers, however, could use iron which enabled them to make more effective weapons and better farming implements such as stronger plough shares. These superior farming implements allowed them to till parts of the land that had not been exploited before. The origins of the stories which were recorded later as the *Iliad* and *Odyssey* date back to this period and are 'epic' poems that had been passed down orally through the centuries.

By 800BC, with the improved agricultural methods, there was a population explosion and the rise of a vigorous new culture. Farming stimulated the growth of self-contained city states, each consisting of a town with its surrounding countryside. The boom in population and the need to trade prompted the Greeks to travel farther afield and colonies were formed in North Africa, Sicily, southern Italy and southern France. Their Near Eastern contacts influenced the Greek art, but more importantly, the Greeks acquired an alphabet, adapted from that of the Phoenicians, which brought literacy back to Greece and saw the flowering of the earliest Greek poetry we know today — Homer and Heriod.

The many city states had their own varied traditions and therefore had different legends and myths. They also had their own singular forms of government. The two most powerful states were Sparta and Athens. Sparta, in particular, was quite unlike any other state with its severe regime designed solely to produce soldiers. Athens, whose wealth derived from a natural harbour and silver mines, had a democracy and although citizens had the right to attend a monthly assembly and to vote on matters of the city, only adult men born in the city were eligible 'citizens'.

In 490BC the Persians invaded Greece but were defeated at the battle of Marathon. Ten years later they invaded again, this time winning the battle of Thermoplae, where 300 Spartans and their allies were killed. But the Spartan holding action allowed the Athenians time to organise their defences and, although the Persians occupied Athens, they were finally defeated at the naval battle of Salamis.

BELOW: An example of early Hellenistic sculpture, a pale terracotta head of a horse. Christie's Images

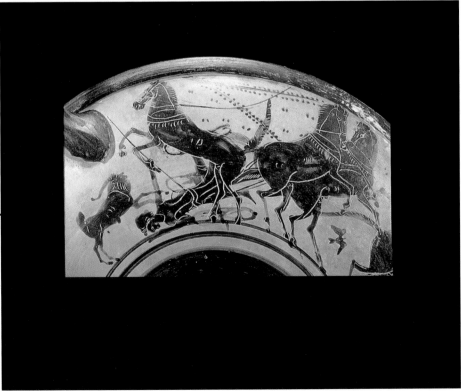

ABOVE: A black figure skyphos, an early example of Ancient Greek art. Christie's Images

LEFT: On this black figure drinking cup an Attic four-horse chariot is depicted toppled on the ground before reaching the finishing post in a race. Christie's Images

ABOVE: The death of Socrates after the artist Rosa Salvator. The famous Greek philosopher died by drinking hemlock after being condemned to death in 599BC. Christie's Images

ABOVE RIGHT: Alexander the Great rewarding his generals after one of his succesful campaigns (after the artist Fernando Francesco Calle D Imperiali). Christie's Images

BELOW RIGHT: The Olympieion or temple of Olympian Zeus — the largest temple in Greece, which took over 700 years to build. It was started by the tyrant Peisistratos and finished in AD131 by the Roman Emperor Hadrian, whose arch defines the split between the classical Greek city and that of Rome. Life-File/Wayne Shakell

After the Persian defeat Athens became leader of an alliance set up to defend the city states against the possibility of further Persian attack. States contributed funds to be used specifically to drive the Persians from the Greek cities of Asia Minor. The Athenians instead used part of this money to build the Parthenon on the Athenian Acropolis — the temple of Athene, the city goddess. Apart from Athens and Sparta the other key city states in classical Greece were Delphi, Olympia, Corinth, Thebes and Argos.

As Athens became more powerful and exerted control over the other Greek states it inevitably came into conflict with Sparta. This led to the Peloponnesian War which lasted for over 25 years until Sparta defeated Athens in 404BC. The warring wasn't confined to just Athens and Sparta, the fighting spread across the whole of the Greek peninsula. This protracted and exhausting war left all the states involved very depleted and unstable. Sparta finally emerged as the ruling power amongst the Greeks and, with their oligarchic political system and hatred of democracy, they abused their power and many democrats were killed.

The other city states rebelled against them and in 371BC Thebes rose up and defeated Sparta. For a short while Thebes dominated Greece but then another damaging conflict amongst the states broke out. The ensuing weakness of the states enabled King Philip of Macedon to take advantage of the situation and take control of Greece through force of arms..

Macedonia lay to the north-east of Greece and had gained wealth from the gold mines of Mt Pangaeus. It was still a monarchy, a form of government derided by the Greeks as barbaric, indeed they barely considered the Macedonians to be Greek at all. Under Philip, Macedonia grew strong and developed a well trained army. In 338BC he advanced to central Greece and defeated the Thebans and the Athenians but when he returned to Macedon in 336BC he was murdered. Philip's plan to extend the influence of Macedonia into Asia Minor and beyond was left to his son to carry out; his son was to become one of the most glorified icons of the western world — Alexander the Great.

Alexander was just 20 years old when he and his well trained and loyal army invaded Asia Minor in 334BC. From an early age he had been trained in Spartan ways and, when he was only 13 years old, Aristotle the great Athenian philosopher became his teacher. Alexander's campaign to extend the Macedonian Empire took his armies as far afield as India and Egypt. During the 11-year campaign he defeated every great nation against whom he led his army and was planning a campaign to Arabia when he died in Babylon in 323BC. After his death Alexander's empire was divided into kingdoms ruled by his former generals — and for many years wars raged across Greece and the Near East as they each tried to establish control.

Alexander's empire and Greek culture dominated the known world and heralded the 'Hellenistic Age' after the Greek name for their country. This physical domination was to last until 146BC when the expanding Roman Empire extended its dominion over Greece and the city states had all been destroyed. Culturally the Romans were to adopt much in art, science and mythology from the Hellenistic world which they took back with them to the west.

Structure of Greek Mythology and Religion

BELOW: At a time when a trireme cost 5 talents the sum of 8,000 talents was riches beyond compare! When that sum was lodged by the Delian League in the Acropolis, Pericles — the dominant personality in Athens from 455 to 429BC — saw the chance to make Athens the beacon for all Greeks. The Parthenon would cost just over 2,000 talents. Its eight massive end and 17 side columns are immensely sophisticated works of Doric architecture with a bulge in the centre, an inclination of the corner columns (which are also imperceptibly wider than the others) and a slight curving of the horizontal lines — all to compensate for the optical illusions created by such massive stonework. Of course when it was built it would not have been the colour it is today: ancient civilisations painted and decorated their temples and the areas around would have been thronged by statues and shrines to cults. By 438BC the 50ft statue of Athena — made from gold and ivory and itself costing 700 talents — would have stood inside.
Life-File/F. Ralston

THE religion of Mycenae did not survive the Dark Age which followed the collapse of the civilisation.But from the 8th century BC the work of the epic poets helped to soldify what had become a set of local traditions and beliefs. As with so many ancient religions, the Greeks did not have the trappings of religion so common today — a written liturgy or body of canon law. Most of the priesthood were ordinary citizens elected for a period of time — usually a year.

In common with other religions the Greeks did not distinguish between mythology and ancient history, almost all their heroes, from whom they believed they were descended, were themselves related to the gods. The ancient Greek religion was polytheistic, like many civilisations of ancient times the people believed in more than one god; but as the expanding Greek city states absorbed their smaller neighbours together with their local deities, they set up an official state cult of the Olympian gods to express this new sense of unity. Although all were revered, different cities had different individual gods as their special patrons. Apollo's shrine at Delphi, however, was recognised throughout the Greek world.

The Greeks believed it was the gods who made the sun rise and set, the rains fall and the crops grow. They personified many of these natural phenomena with, for example, Iris being the rainbow and Hyperion being the sun. Their religion or mythology were the stories handed down of how the gods were supposed to make things happen. There was a strong involvement between the gods and man and cults concerning life's unpredictability — like that of Fortune. Although the gods were omnipotent to the Greeks they were by no means above criticism. In the late 6th century BC, at the height of the oracle at Delphi, there was certainly articulate criticism of the amorality of the Olympian gods. The Greeks were, however, also very careful to thank the gods for good fortune by offering them gifts and making sacrifices to them. Apart from the large temples built in honour of the various gods, pious Greeks dedicated small bronze statues in their homes and shrines in gratitude of favours received or in the hope of favours to come.

There are various Greek myths which bear a strong resemblance to other foundation stories and religions, notably their story of Deucalion's Flood which shows a close approximation to the story of Noah in the Old Testament. Olympia, the home of the gods, is sometimes called 'Heaven' in Greek mythology. It is not, however, somewhere the souls of mortals can go unless they have been deified. The nearest the ancient Greeks came to an idea of a resting place for the souls of man was in their mythology of the Underworld, Tartarus. The stories here embodied some idea of reincarnation. The Orchards of Elysium, which are ruled over by Cronus, lie near Hades' dominions but form no part of them. Elysium is a paradise of continuous sunshine and happiness where inhabitants may elect to be reborn on earth whenever they please. Nearby are the Fortunate Islands reserved for those that have been three times born and three times attained Elysium.

Outside Hades palace were the Asphodel Fields where all the dead souls

ABOVE: Alexander the Great and his doctor Philip, after Théodore Géricault. Christie's Images

would meet and where the souls of the undistinguished would wander without purpose for eternity. At a junction of three roads, close to the Asphodel Fields, the souls of the dead would be judged and their eternal fate decided. If they were found not to have been particularly heroic or virtuous but had not been evil they were sent back to the Asphodel Fields: if, however, they were judged to have been depraved and immoral they were sent to the punishment fields of Tartarus to suffer eternal torment. The third route was reserved for the real heroes, those that had led honourable and courageous lives; they were sent to the Orchards of Elysium

Despite the efforts of poets and philosophers the Greek gods never lost their essentially anthropomorphic character and Greek religion largely lacked the insistence on the high standards of personal morality associated with Christianity, Islam and Judaism. It also had no really developed concept of an 'after life'. Furthermore its influence was weakened by some of the more mystical aspects of Near East religion, especially in the period after Alexander's conquests of Asia Minor and Egypt. It finally fell victim first to Christianity and then to Islam.

Creation Myths and Main Stories

OVERLEAF: *Prometheus bound to a rock with a vulture pecking at his liver after an artist of the Italian Flemish School (1600). The attraction of classical subjects was reborn in the 15th century when the Renaissance — literally rebirth — took place. Prometheus, undergoing dreadful torment awaiting his saviour Heracles, was also the subject of a famous lyrical drama by Shelley, the title of which — Prometheus Unbound — mirrors the tale of Prometheus Bound by the great Athenian tragic poet Aeschylus.*
Christie's Images

THE schematic creation myth has at the beginning Chaos; from Chaos came a daughter, Earth, and Night. Earth's husband was Heaven (Uranus). Earth first produced the Sea then Oceanus (Ocean) which is the stream which encircles the Earth and beyond which no man can go. Earth then produced the Titans and the Cyclopes. Many of the Titans are nothing more than personifications: Mnemosyne is Memory (mother of the Muses); Hyperion is the Sun and Phoebe the Moon. There are hints in the *Iliad* and the *Odyssey* that Ocean 'the source of the gods' may have once played a larger role in an alternative myth. The idea that all things arose out of the sea is not exactly an uncommon hypothesis and is paralleled in many other cosmogenies.

After the creation myth the origin and genealogy of the gods became more humanistic. The myth of Cronus, the youngest of the Titans, illustrates this. Uranus hated his children and, as they were born, hid them away. Earth, their mother, devised a scheme to allow her children to take revenge on their father. Cronus was the only one courageous enough to carry out the plan. Earth took Cronus to her bed armed with a sickle. When Uranus returned, bringing Night with him, he stretched out on Earth. Cronus then took the sickle and castrated him flinging the parts upon the Earth. From the blood that gushed over Earth she eventually bore the Furies and the Titans.

This classical Oedipal fantasy in which the child succeeds in supplanting the father in his mother's bed suggests this myth arose about 1000BC when the Dorians entered Greece. The Dorians' social organisation was based upon the small nuclear family in which an autocratic father rules the marriage. In this type of family, where all authority derives from the father who alone enforces the moral sanctions, a child can be made to feel guilty. This guilt can lead to the child hating his father. Prior to the Dorians the social organisation was based on an extended family where a child is brought up in an atmosphere of approval or disapproval. The child's behaviour is judged by all the members of the extended family — brothers, sisters, aunts, uncles and cousins — and will be rewarded or shamed accordingly. The Oedipal element, along with homicides, seductions and incest, appears throughout Greek mythology.

The second part of the Greek succession myth concerns Zeus, the high god of the Greeks. Rhea, a Titan, bore Cronus a number of children — Hestia, Demeter, Hera and Hades. Fearing that he would eventually be supplanted by his son, he swallowed these children. When the youngest, Zeus, was about to be born Uranus and Earth sent Rhea to Crete where she had the child in a cave. Earth tricked Cronus into believing he had swallowed Zeus by giving him a stone wrapped in swaddling clothes. Zeus grew rapidly and, with the help of Earth, overthrew Cronus who vomited up all his children along with the stone he had swallowed. The analogous Babylonian myth had Zeus (or his equivalent) slit open his father with a sword. The Greek myth concentrates its attention upon the stone which is identified as the sacred stone of Delphi. Zeus sent two eagles flying, one from the east and one from the west, they met over Delphi which was chosen as the site and became an important cult centre and oracle.

Zeus, the newly triumphant god, now had to defend his position against the Titans who resented the overthrow of their brother Cronus. The battle that Zeus and the younger gods, his brothers and sisters, fought against the Titans lasted 10 years. It was on the plains of Thessaly that the Titans were defeated and possession of Olympus, the home of the gods, gained.

It is common in mythology for great enterprises to be completed with the aid of outside agencies, a 'helper' or 'helpers', often specially endowed with particular talents or weapons. Earth at this stage was still on the side of Zeus. Earth advised Zeus to enlist the help of the 'Hundred Handers', three of her children by Uranus who had never been released. It was their ability to throw 300 rocks at once which helped Zeus to rout the Titans and pursue them to Tartarus, the Underworld.

Earth was so upset by this treatment of the Titans, who were, after all, also her children, that she once again changed sides. She bore another son, her youngest, called Typhon. It was expected that he would continue the succession. Urged on by Earth, Typhon fought a terrible series of battles with Zeus. It was against Typhon that Zeus used thunderbolts, made for him by his armourers the Cyclopes, for the first time. As their battle raged across Greece and into Thrace, Typhon picked up whole mountains and hurled them at Zeus. The power of Zeus's thunderbolts rendered this useless and the mountains shattered and rebounded on Typhon. Zeus eventually chased Typhon to Sicily and in one final battle hurled Mount Etna upon him, pinning him under it. The eruptions of the volcano were said to be Typhon's attempts to free himself. This version of the creation myth firmly established Zeus as the surviving and victorious high god of the Greeks.

There does not seem to be any definitive story connected with the creation of man in Greek mythology. Early Greeks seem to have supposed that man, animals and plants merely sprang from the ground. There was an Olympian myth concerning the five 'ages of man' saying that Earth bore men spontaneously. The first age of man was the golden race — the subjects of Cronus who were more akin to immortals than mere men. They led a carefree, gentle life without wars or disputes. They eventually disappeared but their spirits remained to give hope and high moral aspirations to mankind. After the golden race came the silver race. These were also divinely created and, although they too never made war upon each other, they were quarrelsome and ignorant. Zeus got rid of them because they never made sacrifices to the gods.

The third age of men was the bronze race armed with bronze weapons. This was a violent and cannibalistic race which revelled in death and war. Death soon overtook them. The fourth race of men was also a bronze race. It was, however a much nobler and heroic race than its predecessor. This was the race that was written about in the early myths and stories. It provided the brave heroes of the Trojan War, the Argonauts and the other great characters of Greek legend whose souls

ABOVE: A Hellenistic terracota figure of the winged goddess Nike, the personification of victory. She was, according to Hesiod, the daughter of the Titan Pallas and Styx — the eldest daughter of Oceanus and Tethys after whom the underworld river was named — but supported the Olympians in their battle against the Titans. It was Nike who escorted Heracles to Olympus after he was deified. Christie's Images

Seen from the Parthenon, the Erechtheion was completed later — in 407BC — in the Ionic style, next to the old temple of Athene which was destroyed by the Persians. Dedicated to Athena and Poseidon-Erechtheus, it commemorates the contest the god and goddess had for possession of the Acropolis. In the contest Athena caused an olive tree to sprout from the rock (the one you can see on the Acropolis today was planted by an American archaeologist) and Poseidon a seawater spring. The Gods decided that Athena was the victor and so the Acropolis was dedicated to Athene Promachus — Athena the Champion. Whether the Erechtheion derives from the spring — Erechtheis — or an older king of Athens, is debated. On the south side (nearest the camera) is the Porch of the Caryatids who hold the entabulature on their heads. They are modelled on the widows of Carya, a city punished for its alliance with the Persians. The caryatids there today are replacements: two are in the Acropolis Museum, a third in the British Museum. Life-File/Sue Davies

reside in the Elysian Fields. The fifth age of man, according to this creation myth, was the present one. This 'iron' race was brutal and decadent and totally unworthy of their heroic forebears

There is a later tradition concerning the origins of man which suggests that Prometheus, one of the Titans, made man out of clay into which the goddess Athene breathed life. He made him in the image of the gods and gave him an upright stature so that, whilst all the other animals looked downwards, man raised his face to the heavens and gazed upon the stars. Prometheus was brother to Epimetheus, Atlas and Menoetius. Whereas Atlas and Menoetius had sided with Cronus in the battle for Olympus, the more prudent Prometheus had persuaded his brother Epimetheus to fight on Zeus's side. Zeus killed Menoetius with his thunderbolts but spared Atlas, the war leader of the Titans, for a special punishment. Zeus condemned him to hold the earth and heaven upon his shoulders for eternity.

Meanwhile, Athene taught Prometheus many skills and arts which he passed on to mankind. Zeus was getting concerned about the growing knowledge and power of man and Prometheus was aware of this. Of all the things Zeus had expressly forbidden it was giving mankind the wonderful but potentially dangerous gift of fire. Prometheus chose to ignore Zeus; he lit a glowing ember from the chariot of the sun god and hid it away from the sight of Zeus in a giant fennel stalk which he then delivered to man. Zeus was furious and he ordered Hephaestus to make a woman out of clay. The winds breathed life into the woman and the goddesses dressed and adorned her. Zeus named this beautiful woman Pandora. He gave her a box into which he had put, unknown to her, all the evils and ills that might beset mankind and delivered her to Epimetheus to take as a wife.

Prometheus had warned his brother not to accept gifts from the devious Zeus. When Epimetheus declined the hand of Pandora in marriage Zeus's revenge on Prometheus was terrible. He had him chained to a mountain in the Caucasus where a voracious vulture pecked away all day at his liver.

There was no end to this infernal torment as his liver rejuvenated every night leaving the torture to start anew the next day. Epimetheus, horrified and terrified by his brother's fate, quickly agreed to marry Pandora. Zeus had made Pandora almost as stupid as she was beautiful and he knew that, although he had forbidden her to open the box, her curiosity would get the better of her. Pandora and Epimetheus opened it and all the evils and ill spirits descended upon mankind. They quickly shut the box managing to keep Hope which enabled mankind to persevere and survive.

Zeus was getting increasingly impatient with mankind for its violent and ignorant nature and its lack of due respect to himself and the other gods. He decided to pay a visit to earth to see for himself what was going on. He disguised himself as a poor beggar for the visit. He was treated with great disdain wherever he went and was appalled by the hospitality he received. He swore to make mankind pay for this disgraceful treatment. On his return to Mount Olympus he sent a great flood upon the earth. Storms raged, thunder crashed and lightening struck the whole land. Streams became rivers, rivers became torrents and gradually the sea level began to rise. Deucalion, the son of Prometheus, had been warned of the flood by his father. He built an ark for himself and his wife Pyrrha. As the seas rose, covering the entire land, the two of them were safe. Eventually all that remained above sea level were the tops of the highest mountain peaks and it seemed as though all mortal life had perished except Deucalion and Pyrrha. In time the rains stopped and their ark came to rest on Mount Parnassus.

When Deucalion and Pyrrha disembarked on to the dry land they made a sacrifice to Zeus in gratitude for their saviour and pleaded with him to restore mankind. Zeus was moved by their pitiful but earnest lament and sent Hermes to reassure them that their plea would be answered. Hermes told them that they must cast the bones of their dead mother to the ground. They understood mother to mean mother earth, and the bones to be the rocks that were strewn upon the ground around them. They picked up the rocks and cast them over their shoulders. As each rock hit the ground a man or woman immediately sprang up, a man if Deucalion had thrown the rock, a woman if it was Pyrrha. In this way mankind was restored.

A 19th Century French cast iron figure depicting the personification of Hope, all that was left in Pandora's box after it was opened. Christie's Images

THE TROJAN WAR AND THE TRAVELS OF ODYSSEUS

Greek legends tell of a 10-year war between the Greeks and the people of Troy in Asia Minor. Homer's Iliad is a poem about this war and the people involved in it. Troy was said to have been founded by a man called Teucer who became its first king and under his great-great-grandson, Ilos, it received the name Ilium.

According to legend, the son of Ilos was Laomedon, who was regarded as a cheat and a liar. Apollo and Poseidon built a wall round Troy for him, but Laomedon refused to give them the payment he had promised. In revenge the gods sent a sea monster to ravage Troy but the hero Heracles promised to kill it on the condition that Laomedon gave him his horses. Heracles killed the monster but, once again, Laomedon broke his word. In a rage Heracles sacked Troy and killed Laomedon. He did, however, spare Laomedon's son, Priam, who was king of Troy at the time of the Trojan War.

The cause of the war was an event at the wedding of the Nereid Thetis and Peleus, a prince of Thessaly. During the wedding festivities the uninvited Eris, goddess of Discord and the sister of Ares (god of War), threw down an apple which was inscribed 'for the fairest'. The goddesses Hera, Athene and Aphrodite who were attendant at the wedding all claimed the apple. It was decided that a Trojan prince called Paris should arbitrate and choose 'the fairest' in what became known as the 'Judgment of Paris'. Paris was the son of Priam, the king of Troy, and Hecuba. When he was a baby Paris's mother Hecuba dreamt that he would one day cause the destruction of Troy so she took him to the hills and abandoned him. He was found and brought up by some shepherds until he was eventually reclaimed by Priam.

Each of the three goddesses attempted to bribe Paris; Hera offered him power and promised to make him ruler of all Europe and Asia Minor; Athene offered him wisdom saying he would become a great soldier and statesman who would lead Troy to victory over the Greeks; Aphrodite offered him the most beautiful woman

'Was this the face that launch'd a thousand ships, and burnt the top-less towers of Ilium?'
The elopement of Helen with Paris of Troy has been an inspiration to artists since Homer. Here, The Rape of Helen *after the artist Hans Jordaens (1595 - 1643) shows the abduction of Helen by the Trojans — the starting point of the Trojan War.*
Christie's Images

in the world. Paris chose Aphrodite. The woman Aphrodite chose for Paris was Helen, a daughter of Zeus and a Spartan princess called Leda whom Zeus had seduced when he came to her in the disguise of a swan. Helen was already married to Menelaus, the king of Sparta, when Paris came to his court and abducted her.

Menelaus called for the aid of his brother Agamemnon, the king of Mycenae, and asked for as many Greek heroes as he could muster to sail in pursuit of Paris to Troy where Helen had been taken. Amongst the heroes who sailed to the siege of Troy was Achilles, the son of Thetis and Peleus, who was considered to be the greatest warrior of them all. The guile of the expedition was to be provided by Odysseus and the wise Nestor.

It was a formidable fleet and army which left the Greek shores to embark on the siege of Troy. The walled Trojan city, with its wise king Priam and his courageous son Hector, was equal to the Greeks. They camped on the plains outside Troy for years with the occasional skirmishes taking place outside the city walls. Occasionally the gods would intervene in events; Athene and Hera, still smarting from the judgment of Paris, supported the Greeks whilst Apollo and Aphrodite were on the side of the Trojans. In a dreadful and bloody fight Achilles slew Priam's son Hector and dragged the body three times round the city walls behind his chariot to taunt the Trojans but still they would not give up. After Achilles was slain by Paris, shot in his vulnerable heel, and then Paris was himself killed by the Greek hero Philoctetes, Odysseus decided it was time to use some guile.

He instructed the carpenter Epeius to build a large wooden horse with the

The Trojan hero Hector and the Greek hero Ajax during their day long battle. At nightfall they recognised each other as equal adversaries and exchanged gifts. Unfortunately Hector's duel with Achilles would not end so happily and Hector's dead body would be dragged behind the Greek's chariot around the walls of Troy. Christie's Images

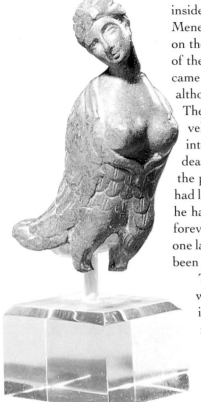

*A Roman bronze
statuette of a siren. Half bird and half
woman, the sirens sang so sweetly to
sailors that they forgot everything and
were lured to their death. Odysseus —
Ulysses in the Roman version — lis-
tened to the song but lashed himself to
the mast of his ship to save complica-
tions! His companions were given the
infinitely more sensible, if painful,
treatment to stop them succumbing —
their ears were filled with wax. In
Homer's mythology there were only two
sirens; later writers added more.*
Christie's Images

inside hollowed out and big enough to carry armed soldiers. Odysseus, Epeius and Menelaus were among the men who climbed into the wooden horse which was left on the open plain outside Troy. With the exception of a man called Sinon the rest of the Greek fleet sailed away apparently having given up the siege. The Trojans came out of their city and stared in wonderment at the giant wooden horse and, although some were suspicious of it, others wanted to drag it inside the city walls.

The biggest voice of dissent came from Laocoön, a priest of Apollo, who argued vehemently against taking this 'gift' into the city. The gods on the Greek side intervened and sent two giant serpents to crush Laocoön and his two sons to death. The Trojans took this as proof that the horse was a sacred object which the priest had insulted and to convince them further Sinon, the man the Greeks had left behind, was discovered and brought before King Priam. He told them that he had deserted the Greeks and that if they took the horse into the city it would forever protect Troy. As they dragged the horse through the city gates there was one last voice of caution. This came from Cassandra, a daughter of Priam, who had been given the gift of prophesy but was destined never to be believed.

That night when the Trojans were feasting and celebrating Sinon crept to the wooden horse and undid the hidden trapdoor which released the armed men inside. The Greeks began sacking the city and lit beacons on the city walls to recall their fleets which had not sailed home but had merely hidden on the nearby island of Tenedos. King Priam took refuge at the altar of Zeus but was slain by Neoptolemus the son of Achilles. One of the Trojans who did escape was a son of Aphrodite, Aeneas, whose travels and eventual arrival in Italy where he was said to be founder of Rome are recounted in Virgil's Aeneid .

When the Greek king Agamemnon returned home he found that his wife Clytemnestra, sister of Helen, had taken a lover. The pair then murdered Agamemnon. Clytemnestra's son Orestes was later to avenge his father's murder by in turn killing his mother. Menelaus, on the other hand, lived happily for many years with Helen whom he had rescued in Troy and brought back to Sparta.

ODYSSEUS

AFTER the Trojan war Odysseus set sail with his fleet of ships and their crews for their home of Ithaca. It was, however, going to be some time before he arrived home. The stories of his great adventures are told in Homer's Odyssey. The Odyssey begins with a meeting of the gods in heaven to decide whether he should be allowed to return home after all his wanderings. The reason why he was always being blown off course and shipwrecked and why it took him 10 years to get home from Troy was that he had become a pawn in a battle between two factions of the Olympian gods.

He had only just left Troy when Poseidon intervened and caused the winds to blow his ships off course. They came to the Land of the Lotus Eaters where some of his crew ate the fruit of the lotus. The fruits contained a potent soporific which made the sailors forget who they were and what they were doing and it was only through force that Odysseus could coerce his men back to their ships. Having escaped these lands they next came to the isle of the Cyclops, one eyed giants, and sons of the original Cyclopes. They were captured by Polyphemus, one of these monsters, and kept in his cave where he had killed and eaten six of Odysseus's men before he contrived a plan to escape. Whilst the Cyclops was asleep in a drunken stupor Odysseus put out his one eye with a wooden stake. They managed to make their escape as the blinded giant blundered around in an agonised but furious rage.

The Cyclops hurled rocks at the ships as they sailed away bound this time for the god of the winds. Here Odysseus was given a bag which contained all the unfavourable winds that might hinder him on his return to Ithaca. It took just 10 days to reach sight of the land of Ithaca but the curiosity of some of the crew led them to open the bag containing the winds. As they opened it a mighty tempest sprang up and blew the fleet far away from their homelands to the isle of the Laistrygonian cannibals where all but Odysseus, with his ship and crew, perished. They next arrived at the home of the enchantress Circe on the island of Aeaea. Circe was a daughter of the sun god and had the powers to turn men into wild animals. When some of the crew accepted her invitation to a feast she turned them into pigs. With the aid of a special herb, given to him by Hermes, Odysseus managed to persuade Circe to restore his crew but it was to be a year before they left Aeaea.

Odysseus now went to the Underworld to seek the counsel of the soul of the dead prophet Teiresias who warned him of the many dangers he still faced and advised him on how to overcome them. Among the dangers he encountered were the Sirens, beautiful enchantresses, whose ethereal singing lured sailors to their death on the rocks. Odysseus overcame their temptations by plugging the ears of his crew with wax to make them deaf to their haunting strains before having them lash him to the mast of his ship so that he could enjoy their singing without endangering himself.

They endured many perils but Odysseus himself always remained safe. He successfully navigated the narrow strait guarded by the sea monster Scylla on the one side and the fatal whirlpool Charybdis on the other. On the coast of Sicily his crew disobeyed him and ate some cattle, an act he had expressly forbidden. These cattle belonged to the god Apollo who took a mighty vengeance on them by striking the ship with a lightning bolt that hurled all the crew overboard to their deaths. Odysseus alone survived and after days drifting on the open sea was washed up

The Temple of Poseidon in Athens at sunset. Poseidon, the god of the sea, was one of the great gods and became Neptune in Roman mythology. He helped Apollo build the walls of Troy but then, in a change of sides so usual in Greek mythology and politics, sided with the Greeks against Troy because the Trojans refused him his reward.
Life-File/Jeremy Hoare

on the shores of the isle of Orygia, home of Calypso a nymph and daughter of Atlas.

Odysseus's chief ally on Olympus was Athene. After the meeting of the gods which starts Homer's Odessey she went straight to Ithaca to give advice to Odysseus's son Telemachus. Telemachus and Penelope, Odysseus's wife, were in difficulties because a large number of neighbouring chieftains had gathered in Odysseus's land telling Penelope that he was dead and that she must choose one of them as a new husband. These chiefs were envious of Odysseus's holdings and saw a way of gaining it through marriage to Penelope. She tried to put them off by pretending to be making a wedding dress which was taking an age to complete. It was a great relief when Athene came, disguised as an old friend of Odysseus, to suggest that Telemachus should set out to find news of his father. This journey, on which Athene went with Telemachus, helped to postpone any decision Penelope might have to make about a possible suitor. The potential candidates were infuriated and they plotted to kill Telemachus on his return. Journeying through Greece Telemachus heard at last, from Menelaus, that his father was alive on Calypso's island and that the gods had ordered Calypso to set him free.

Odysseus spent seven years with Calypso until Zeus commanded her to help him build a ship with which to depart. As he left Orygia the wrathful sea god Poseidon intervened once more by blowing up a great storm which wrecked the ship, but once again Odysseus escaped death and was washed up on the shores of Scheria where he was found by the king's daughter Nausicaa. It was at the court of King Alcinous that he told of all the trials and tribulations his epic journey from Troy had brought him. The king took great pity on him and provided him with a new ship and crew to enable him to get home to Ithaca. This time he did make it home and, on reaching the shores of Ithaca, the crew laid him asleep on the sands before sailing away. When he awoke Athene was there to tell him of the dangers that faced Telemachus and Penelope and of the plotting of his wife's suitors. Odysseus disguised himself as a beggar whilst Athene went off to fetch Telemachus. He arrived at his own court where the suitors, taking him to be the beggar he looked, taunted and ridiculed him. Telemachus was the only one who knew his true identity and even Penelope failed to recognise him. Thinking that her husband must truly be dead she finally agreed to take one of the suitors. She offered her hand to any one of them who could shoot a single arrow from Odysseus's bow through a row of 12 axe heads. They all failed until the 'beggar' asked for a shot which duly succeeded. Odysseus threw off his disguise and, with the help of Telemachus and Athene, killed all the rival suitors. Penelope finally recognised him and he knew he was at last at home.

JASON AND THE GOLDEN FLEECE

THERE are many versions of the story of the Golden Fleece. The King of Thessaly had a son and a daughter, Phrixus and Helle. He remarried and their stepmother hated the children and wanted them killed. They were saved by a present their own mother had given them, a wonderful ram with a golden fleece. It carried the children on its back away from their stepmother. On the way Helle fell from its back into the water and drowned. Where she fell into the strait between Europe and Asia Minor (the Dardanelles) is still called the Hellespontos or Helle Sea by the Greeks. Phrixus, clinging to the ram, reached safety at Colchis at the eastern end of the Black Sea. He was well treated by the king there and eventually married the princess Chalciope. To give thanks for his escape Phrixus sacrificed the ram to Zeus and hung its fleece in a grove in Colchis guarded by a serpent

Back in Thessaly the king died and his nephew Aeson became king only to be driven out by his own stepbrother Pelias. When Aeson's son Jason grew up he came to Pelias and demanded his father's kingdom back. Pelias recognised Jason as the stranger that the oracle had foretold would kill him. He challenged Jason to fetch the Golden Fleece which he knew would be an extremely dangerous task. If Jason were to return with the fleece he could have his kingdom back. Jason agreed and gathered heroes from all parts of Greece to sail with him on his ship the Argo; the crew were known as the Argonauts. According to different stories the Argonauts had many different compositions. Families in Ancient Greece liked to claim descent from an Argonaut so, as the legends grew, so did the number of Argonauts. Ancient Greek history and their mythology were once again one and the same thing.

Jason encountered many adventures on the way to Colchis including a long stay on the island of Lemnos where the women, and their queen Hypsipele, had murdered their husbands and were only too eager to welcome a party of men. They also rescued the blind seer Phineus from the Harpies. The Argonauts came to the island where Phineus lived. He had upset the gods by having the ability to forecast the future too accurately so for this 'crime' they blinded him, furthermore to add to his torment he was being plagued by a pair of Harpies! These were grotesque bird-like monsters with women's faces.who would swoop on Phineus whilst he was dining, clawing at his face, and stealing his food. When Jason asked Phineus for advice on how to find and retrieve the Golden Fleece he agreed provided they first rid him of the Harpies. Calais and Zeteus — winged sons of the north wind Boreas — were entrusted with the task of getting rid of them. In the evening when they all sat down to dine the shrieking Harpies descended upon them pecking and scratching at the table. The two winged Argonauts unsheathed their swords and flew at the Harpies driving them far out to sea. Phineus then told Jason how to navigate the Bosphorus and, with his gift of prophesy, told him exactly what he could expect on the way to Colchis. One of the dangers facing the Argonauts were the 'wandering rocks' which guarded the entrance to the Bosphorus; they successfully navigated their way through these rocks which have since been rationalised as ice-floes in the Black Sea coming down from frozen Russian rivers.

The Argo eventually arrived at Colchis where the king told Jason he could have the Golden Fleece if he could perform three tasks. The first task was to plough a field with a pair of fire breathing bulls and sew it with some dragon's teeth which immediately sprang up as fully armed warriors who Jason had to fight and overcome. The king did not believe for one minute that it was possible to successfully achieve these tasks and he might have been right had it not been for the intervention of his daughter, Medea. She despite being a witch and sorceress, she had fallen in love with Jason, and used her many magic powers for his benefit.

With Medea's help Jason completed his tasks and slew the dragon that guarded the grotto where the Golden Fleece hung on a tree. They set sail with the Fleece only to be pursued by the angry king's son but Medea, once again using her magic, slew her brother.

They arrived home to Thessaly to find Aeson still alive but old and very frail. Medea, using her sorcery, rejuvenated the old man by boiling him in a cauldron with some special herbs which brought back his youth and vigour. She then tricked the daughters of Peleas by saying she could do the same for their father but she gave them the wrong herbs and he perished. After this, all interest in the legend shifts to Medea. The manner of Jason's death is briefly told by later story tellers. After wandering around Greece he returns to Corinth where, ironically, he is killed by a piece of the Argo dropping off onto his head.

THE LABOURS OF HERACLES

THE first task Heracles had to perform was to kill and flay the Nemean lion, an enormous beast with a pelt proof against iron, bronze and stone. Heracles waited until the lion returned to its lair then fired a volley of arrows at it. The arrows proved to be ineffective and just bounced off its impenetrable fur. He tried his sword to no avail, it merely bent, and when his club shattered into pieces after a mighty blow on the beast's head he realised weapons would be useless. He grabbed hold of the lion and began to wrestle with it and, although it bit off one of his fingers, he got it in a mighty head lock and choked it to death. Heracles flayed the animal with its own razor sharp teeth and claws and thereafter wore the invulnerable pelt as armour with the beast's head for a helmet.

The Second Labour Heracles was asked to perform was to kill the Lernaean Hydra, an offspring of the Titans Typhon and Echidne. The Hydra was a many-headed monster, with one of the heads being immortal, and was so venomous that even the smell of its breath could prove fatal. Heracles was driven to the Hydra's lair by Iolaus in his chariot. Heracles fired some burning arrows into the monster's den to smoke it out and when it emerged he grabbed hold of it taking care not to inhale any of its breath. Whilst Heracles crushed the many skulls of the Hydra with his trusty club it twined itself around his legs in an attempt to bring him down. When Heracles realised that for every head he battered, two or three more grew in their place, he called out to Iolaus for help asking him to set fire to some bushes. With the blazing branches Iolaus seared the stumps of the crushed heads to prevent any new ones growing and Heracles chopped off the immortal one with a mighty blow of his sword. After burying this head in the ground Heracles immersed the points of his arrows in the monster's blood which henceforth any wound from them was likely to be fatal. When Heracles returned to Eurystheus the king would not accept that this labour had been completed because Heracles had called upon the aid of Iolaus.

Heracles' Third Labour was to try to capture and bring back alive the Ceryneian Hind; this hind was sacred to Artemis being one she had chased to the Ceryneian hill as a child. Heracles was aware of this so, as he didn't want to kill or injure the animal, he pursued it relentlessly for a whole year. When at last he got close enough to the hind he shot it with a single arrow which pinned its forelegs together without drawing blood or damaging the beast. When Artemis admonished Heracles for the ill treatment of her hind he explained his predicament, put the blame on Eurystheus, was forgiven and allowed to take the animal alive to Mycenae.

The Fourth Labour also involved the taking alive of an animal — this time it was the Erymanthian Boar. To take such a large and ferocious beast alive was a task of great difficulty. Heracles chased the boar from a thicket with loud shouts, drove it into a deep snow drift and leapt onto its back. He bound the beast in chains and carried it alive back to Mycenae. It was at this time that he heard of the Argonauts' expedition to Colchis which he immediately joined without waiting to hear further orders from Eurystheus.

On his return Heracles' Fifth Task was to clean out the stables belonging to King Augeas which housed 3,000 oxen and had not been cleaned out for 30 years. The stench from the stables,although not affecting the beasts themselves, spread disease and plague across the entire land. Heracles stated that he could clean the whole yard in a day and would do so in return for a tithe of cattle. Augeas made him swear an oath to accomplish the task and likewise swore to keep his side of the bargain.

With the help of Iolaus, Heracles breached the wall of the yard and diverted two neighbouring rivers so that they rushed through the yard, washed it clean, and went on to cleanse all the valley pastures.restoring the land to health. When Heracles went to Augeas, having completed his task before nightfall, Augeas refused to keep his side of the bargain saying the River-gods had done the work and not Heracles. Eurystheus also refused to count this as a Labour saying that Heracles had done it for reward stating his bargain with Augeas for a tithe of cattle.

Heracles' Sixth Labour was to kill the Stymphalian Birds. These birds would rise to the air in great flocks to kill man and beast by discharging a shower of bronze feathers, which had the effect of a flight of arrows, at the same time dropping their poisonous excrement which blighted the crops. These birds lived on the Stymphalian Marsh which was inaccessible to man. Using a rattle given to him by Athene, Heracles shook it and made such a noise that the birds rose into the air in a great flock. Those that Heracles did not shoot down flew off to the Black Sea where the Argonauts later came across them.

Heracles' Seventh Labour was to capture the Cretan Bull the beast which had sired the Minotaur.and was causing havoc on the island of Crete. Refusing any

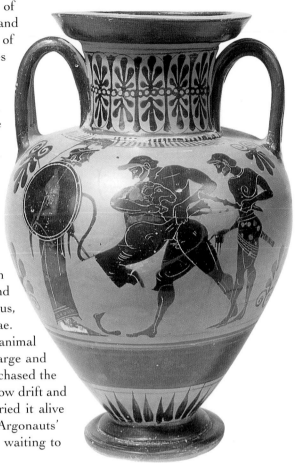

An Attic black figure amphora showing Heracles wrestling with the Nemean Lion. Greek vases come in a variety of shapes and sizes — the large amporae were used mainly for wine or oil. Black-figure work was developed in Corinth and involved incising details on the black silhouette figures and adding white or red paint as necessary. It was overtaken by red-figurework after about 540BC. Christie's Images

Temple of the Olympian Zeus, Athens. Livy said, 'It is the only temple on earth of a size adequate to the greatness of a god.' Reputed to be the biggest temple in Greece, little remains of it and nothing of the two enormous statues of the god and the Emperor Hadrian who dedicated the temple in AD130. By 1450 only 21 columns were still standing; in 1760 the Turkish governor took one to make lime (quite a regular occurrence around Greek temples in Turkish times); a great storm in 1852 blew another down. Today just 16 of the original 104 Corinthian columns still stand.
Life-File/Wayne Shakell

assistance from King Minos, Heracles eventually captured the fire-breathing beast and brought it back to Eurystheus.who released it. The bull roamed across Greece until Theseus captured it, took it to Athens, and sacrificed it to Athene.

Heracles' Eighth Labour was to capture the four savage mares of the Thracian King Diomedes.These were ferocious man-eating beasts which Diomedes used to feed with his unfortunate guests. Heracles overpowered Diomedes's grooms and drove the mares to the shore towards his boat. When Diomedes himself gave chase Heracles stunned him with his club and threw him to his own horses which tore him to pieces and devoured him. With their ravenous hunger satisfied Heracles had little trouble in controlling the mares and brought them back to Mycenae.

Heracles' Ninth Labour was to fetch the girdle of Ares, worn by the Amazonian Queen Hippolyte, for the daughter of Eurystheus. When Heracles reached Themiscyra, where Hippolyte lived, she visited him on his boat, was immediately attracted to him, and would have gladly given him her girdle. However, Hera was going about disguised as an Amazon spreading rumours about the intentions of the strangers and saying that they intended to capture and abduct Hippolyte. The warrior women were incensed and, fully armed, they charged upon Heracles's ship. Heracles now suspecting treachery from the Amazon queen.snatched the girdle from her and killed her.The Amazons fought ferociously and it was only after much slaughter that Heracles managed to sail away and return to Eurystheus with the girdle.

Heracles' Tenth Labour was to fetch the cattle of Geryon,.the King of Tartessus in Spain, who was reputedly the strongest man alive. He had been born with three heads, six hands and three bodies joined together at the waist. His cattle were guarded by the herdsman Eurytion (a son of Ares) and the two headed watchdog Orthrus (born of Typhon and Echidne — as was the Hydra). To reach Tartessus Heracles had to split a mountain in two, thus forming the Strait of Gibraltar. The rocks on either side became known as the 'Pillars of Hercules' (Heracles). When Heracles arrived at Tartessus and approached the cattle the dog Orthrus rushed at him whereupon he dispatched it with one mighty blow of his club. When Eurytion intervened he met the same fate and Heracles began to drive the cattle away. News of this reached Geryon who challenged Heracles to single combat. Heracles fatally shot him, through all three bodies with a single arrow, and successfully embarked on the long and arduous task of driving the cattle home.

Heracles had now performed the Ten Labours which he was expected to do. It had taken him eight years but Eurystheus, discounting the second and the fifth, set him two more. Heracles' Eleventh Labour was to fetch fruit from the Golden Apple tree which Mother Earth had given as a wedding gift to Hera. This tree was planted in Hera's own garden which lay on the slopes of Mount Atlas and was guarded by the dragon Ladon. Heracles had been advised not to try to pick the apples himself but to get the Titan Atlas.to do the job. When Heracles arrived at the garden he asked Atlas to do him this favour. Atlas would have agreed to almost anything to relieve him of his burden of holding the world up but he was afraid of Ladon. When Heracles shot and killed the dragon with an arrow he bent to take the weight of the world on his shoulders whilst Atlas went off to get the apples. Atlas, relieved at having the burden off his back, told Heracles that he would take the apples to Eurystheus himself. Heracles pretended to agree to this but asked Atlas if he would hold up the globe for him for just a few more minutes so he could put a pad on his head to ease the burden.The gullible Atlas put down the apples and resumed his chore. Heracles thanked the Titan, picked up the apples and went on his way.

Heracles' Twelfth and most dangerous task was to bring the dog Cerberus up from Tartarus, the Underworld. Whenever Heracles had got into difficulties, or was exhausted by his tasks, he would invoke Zeus with cries of despair and invariably he would sent Athene down to comfort him. It was in the company of Athene and Hermes that he now descended to Tartarus. When Heracles got to the River Styx his ferocious demeanour frightened the ferryman Charon into rowing him across free of charge.

At the gates of Tartarus Heracles encountered Hades and his wife Persephone. When Heracles demanded the dog Cerburus Hades told him that he could have the beast if he could master it using only his bare hands. The three headed Cerberus had serpents for hair and a vicious barbed tail but Heracles, protected by his lion's pelt, grabbed the beast by the throat and using all his formidable strength never relaxed his grip until the dog yielded. With the aid of Athene, Heracles brought Cerberus up from the Underworld and back to Mycenae. When he arrived Eurystheus, who was offering a sacrifice, handed him a slave's portion. This was too much for Heracles to bear, he had performed his Labours as required, so in a terrible rage of resentment he killed three of Eurystheus's sons.

In the course of completing his tasks, Heracles had performed many other heroic deeds including sailing with the Argonauts in search of the Golden Fleece. Later on he married a princess called Deianira but had many affairs and was generally unfaithful to her. Once, when out with her they came across a swollen river, where the Centaur Nessus offered, for a small fee, to carry Deianira across whilst Heracles swam. Heracles paid Nessus the fare, dived into the river and began to swim across but Nessus, instead of keeping his part of the bargain, galloped off with Deianira and tried to violate her. Heracles, on hearing her cries for help, swam swiftly to the river bank and with his bow pierced Nessus through the breast with an arrow from half a mile away. The dying Nessus told Deianeira that if she mixed his blood with his spilt seed on the ground and soaked Heracles shirt in it he would never be unfaithful to her again. When Heracles did eventually leave Deianeira and put on the fateful shirt he found the blood contained a deadly poison. He tried to tear off the garment but it clung so tightly to him that he tore off pieces of his own flesh. In his agony he built a funeral pyre and threw himself on it. As he burned to death he was born away to Olympus on a cloud and was thus one of the few Greek heroes to be deified.

On the south side of the Erechtheion is the Porch of the Caryatids who hold the entabulature on their heads. They are modelled on the widows of Carya, a city punished for its alliance with the Persians. The caryatids there today are replacements: two are in the Acropolis Museum, a third in the British Museum. Life-File/Jeremy Hoare

Who Was Who in Greek Mythology

Achilles The son of Peleus (King of Thessaly) and the Nereid Thetis, Achilles was regarded as the greatest warrior of the Greek heroes. He brought 50 ships and their men to lay siege on Troy. Achilles fell out with Agamemnon over the Trojan girl Briseis. Achilles had taken the girl captive but Agamemnon, as leader of the Greek forces, took her for himself. The main action of the Iliad centres on Achilles's anger and mortification at this act where he sulks in his tent and comes out to fight again only after his best friend Patroclus is killed. Achilles in grief and anger killed Hector (eldest son of the King of Troy) after chasing him round the walls of Troy. Achilles gave the body of Hector back to Priam only after the funeral of Patroclus. As a baby Achilles was said to have been dipped in the River Styx (the river of the Underworld) by his mother, Thetis, to make him invulnerable. The only part of him that remained dry was where Thetis held him round the ankle. So when Paris shot him in the heel with a poisoned arrow it killed him ('Achilles Heel' — forever after has meant a vulnerable spot). Achilles was said to have been tutored by the Centaur Chiron and is generally remembered for his violent and emotional temperament.

Aeneas Aeneas is a Trojan Hero, son of Anchises (a Trojan Prince) and Aphrodite. In the Iliad he plays only a small part, but later legend has him escape from Troy to become the founder of the Roman people.

Agamemnon The son of Atreus, brother of Menelaus (See House of Pelops) and king of Mycenae. He led the Greek forces in the Trojan War. On his return he was murdered by his wife Clytemnestra and her lover. This act was later avenged by his son Orestes.

Aias, Ajax Aias was a Greek hero depicted as stubbornly courageous but without much of a brain. He recovers the body of Achilles and competes with Odysseus for his armour. Aias loses the competition whereupon he goes mad and kills himself. He does, however, have an alternative end in another story. In this one he drags Cassandra (Priam's daughter) from the altar of Athene and is punished for this

Thetis dipping her infant son Achilles into the river Styx in an attempt to make him invincible (after the artist Antonio Balestra 1666-1740).
Christie's Images

sacrilege by being drowned in a storm sent by the goddess on his journey home to Greece.

Alcinous He is the grandson of Poseidon and husband of his own sister Arete. In the Odyssey he entertains Odysseus and in later legend receives the Argonauts on their return from Colchis. In this legend he also refuses to return Medea to her father. The island of Scheria, where he lived, has been identified as Corfu since classical times.

Amazons The Amazons were a race of mythical female warriors. Their name derives from the practice of amputating their right breasts to make it easier to fire a bow in battle. According to the Iliad King Priam went to war against them but in post Homeric legend they come to aid Troy after the death of Hector where their queen, Penthesilea, was killed by Achilles. Heracles also fought against them after he had killed Hippolyte and taken her girdle (See Heracles). Hippolyte in later legend was the wife of Theseus.

Antigone The daughter of Oedipus, king of Thebes, and his mother Jocasta. Antigone looked after her blinded father in his self impose exile. She returned to Thebes after the deaths of her brothers Eteocles and Polynices. After Oedipus had cursed his sons and departed into exile the brothers agreed to reign alternate years, but Eteocles refused to give up the throne at the end of his year. Polynices gathered together six chieftains to aid him and this was known in Theban legends as the 'Seven against Thebes'. Polynices led his army against the city. In the battle all of the Seven against Thebes, except Adrastus, were killed, as was Eteocles. Adrastus managed to escape thanks to his magic horse, Arion. 10 years later he led the sons of the Seven back to Thebes to avenge their fathers' deaths and sack the city, but died of grief when his own son was killed in battle. On her return to Thebes and after the deaths of her brothers, Antigone committed suicide.

Aphrodite Goddess of beauty, love and reproduction. Aphrodite was worshipped all over Greece but particularly at Paphos in Cyprus, Cythera and Corinth. In primitive legend she is born from the sea foam caused by the castration of Uranus by Cronus and washed ashore at Paphos. According to the Odyssey she is the wife of Hephaestus and the lover of Ares. By her mortal lover, the Trojan Anchises, she is the mother of another Trojan hero, Aeneas. She is also the mother of Eros by Ares.

A Roman marble statue of the Trojan prince Paris. The Romans believed they were descended from the Trojans through the lineage of Aeneas. It was lucky, therefore, that the gods enveloped Aeneas in cloud when he met the invincible Achilles on the Trojan battlefield.
Christie's Images

One of Aphrodite's greatest loves was the mortal Adonis. The wife of the king of Cyprus one day foolishly claimed that her daughter, Smyrna, was even more beautiful than the goddess of love. Aphrodite was incensed by this and came down from Olympus to avenge the insult; she made Smyrna fall hopelessly in love with her father. One night when the king came home so drunk that he did not know what he was doing she climbed into his bed. When he later discovered that the child Smyrna was expecting was not only his grandchild but also his child he flew into an uncontrollable rage. He reached for his sword, but as he attacked his daughter, Aphrodite immediately changed her into a myrrh tree. The blow of the sword cleft the tree in half and from it tumbled the child Adonis.

Aphrodite took care of the child and put him in a chest which she entrusted to Persephone, the queen of Tartarus. Persephone was curious as to the contents of the chest and so opened it to take a look. When she saw Adonis she immediately fell in love with him. Aphrodite heard of this and went down to the Underworld to claim Adonis for herself. Persephone, however, would not agree to the return of Adonis so Aphrodite took her claim to Zeus. This affair proved to be of no interest to Zeus and he handed the arbitration to the Calliope, one of the Muses. Calliope decided that both goddesses had a claim to Adonis and suggested they should share him. She divided the year into three parts, Aphrodite was to have him for one period, Persephone another, and the third would be for Adonis himself to have a rest from the goddesses.

Aphrodite did not play the game with this arrangement. By wearing her magic girdle, which made all fall in love with her, she persuaded Adonis to stay with her all the time thus denying Persephone. Ares, the god of war, was in love with Aphrodite and Persephone saw a way of exploiting this to her own advantage. She went to Ares and told him that Aphrodite much preferred the mortal youth Adonis to himself. Ares was not a god to be messed with and so, when Adonis was out hunting, he changed himself into a wild boar, rushed at the youth, and gored him to death in front of Aphrodite. Where his blood fell upon the earth anemones sprang up.

Aphrodite again went to Zeus and pleaded with him that Adonis should not have to live in the gloom of the Underworld for ever. Zeus relented this time and decreed that Aphrodite should be allowed the company of Adonis during the summer months.

Apollo A symbol of light, youthful manly beauty and reason. Apollo is also associated with music, archery, medicine and prophesy so consequently there are an enormous number of legends which deal with

A Roman bronze figure of Aphrodite — the Greek goddess of love. Christie's Images

his many functions. The island of Delos was sacred to him from earliest times as it was there that the Titan Leto gave birth to him and his twin sister Artemis. When Apollo was still very young he asked for a bow and arrows and set out in pursuit of his mother's deadly enemy Python the serpent. Python had been sent by the jealous Hera in an attempt to kill Leto when she discovered Leto was pregnant by Zeus. Apollo caught up with Python where it lived on Mount Parnassus and severely wounded it with a flight of arrows whereupon it fled to the sacred Oracle at Delphi where the young god killed it.

Apollo was also revered as a god of music after a contest presided over by King Midas in which he beat Pan. Apollo was originally associated with the tending of herds of cattle but this task was taken over by Hermes after he had swapped his tortoiseshell lyre for Apollo's cattle. It was this lyre which Apollo used against Pan's pipes in their musical contest.

Apollo was the first god to fall in love with someone of his own sex namely the beautiful Spartan youth Hyacinthus but it so happened that Zephyrus, the West Wind, was also in love with this youth. One day as Apollo was teaching Hyacinthus to throw the discus the jealous Zephyrus intervened and caused the discus to smash against the youth's head killing him instantly. The Hyacinth flower that grew where his blood lay still carries his initial 'H'.

There were two instances when Apollo incurred the wrath of Zeus, the first was when he had joined Hera's rebellion and the second concerned his son Asclepius who was a great healer. Asclepius had the temerity to bring a mortal back to life and thus rob Hades of a subject. This resurrection so enraged Hades that he put in a complaint to Zeus who acted with typical impetuosity by immediately killing Asclepius by hurling a thunderbolt at him. It was then Apollo's turn to be furious and he turned his anger on the Cyclopes, who had provided Zeus with the thunderbolts, and slew them. If it had not been for the pleading of Apollo's mother, Leto, it is likely that Zeus would have banished him to Tartarus for ever. His sentence was reduced and for the second time he was sentenced to a period of hard labour, the first being when he was sent to assist King Laodon of Troy after the failed Olympian rebellion.

A Roman marble head of the god Apollo, who was, unusually, known by the same name to the Romans as the Greeks. Christie's Images

Ares The Greek god of war possibly imported from Thrace. The Aeropagus, or hill of Ares, was a meeting place for the Greek Council of Elders. Ares was hated by all the other gods except Aphrodite, his sister Eris (Discord) and Hades who was grateful for the souls of soldiers slain in battle. Ares was not an arbitrator and delighted in war and slaughter for its own sake. His sister was the same and positively encouraged dispute and war, this could not have been shown more clearly than her part in the instigation of the Judgment of Paris which led to the Trojan War. Ares was worshipped far more out of fear than anything else, but was never very popular in myth.

Argus Argus was the 100-eyed giant sent by Hera to watch over Io when Zeus turned her into a heifer. Hera had claimed the heifer for herself and told Argus to take it away for safe keeping. When Zeus sent Hermes to fetch it back he knew that he could not steal Io without being detected by one of Argus's 100 eyes so he charmed him to sleep, by the playing of his flute, then cut off his head. Hera placed Argus's eyes in the tail of a peacock as a reminder of his murder.

Ariadne She was the daughter of Minos, King of Crete, who helped guide Theseus through the Labyrinth (See Theseus). Theseus took her away with him but abandoned her on the island of Dia (Naxos). There she was found by Dionysus who married her and gave her a crown of seven stars which became a constellation in the heavens after her death.

Artemis She was probably pre-Olympian in origin, but from Homer onwards was said to be the twin sister of Apollo and was worshipped at Delos with him. She was a virgin huntress associated with wild animals and often referred to as the Moon goddess. With her arrows she brought natural death and punished impiety. The Temple of Diana or Artemesium at Ephesus was one of the Seven Wonders of the Ancient World.

When Artemis was still young her father Zeus asked her what gifts she might like. Like Hestia and Athene she asked that she may remain a virgin and she declared that she only wanted one city but asked for all the mountains in the world as that was where she intended to reside. Zeus gave her many cities and made her the patron of all the roads and harbours of these cities. She also said she wanted a bow and arrows like her twin brother Apollo so he sent her to his armourers the Cyclopes. They made her a silver bow and a quiver full of silver arrows in return for which they could have the first prey she brought down with them. Armed with her new weapons she went to Arcadia where the god Pan gave her a pack of large ferocious hunting hounds.

A Hellenistic bronze statuette, inlaid with silver, of Artemis, twin-sister of Apollo and known to the Romans as Diana — the goddess of hunting. Christie's Images

Artemis demanded the same chastity from her companions that she practised herself and in one instance, on discovering that one of them was pregnant, set her hounds on her to tear her to pieces. The intervention of Zeus who was the father of the unborn child saved the unfortunate woman. The youth Acteon was not so fortunate; he was out hunting one day when he came to a stream where Artemis was bathing and, instead of turning away, he stayed and gazed upon her nakedness. Artemis caught Acteon peeping at her and being afraid that he would brag about seeing a goddess in this way she brought a terrible punishment upon him. She changed him into a stag whereupon his own pack of 50 hounds tore him to pieces.

Asclepius A Greek hero and god of Healing. He is the son of a Thessalian princess, Coronis, and Apollo. During her pregnancy Coronis fell in love with an Arcadian youth. Apollo was told this by a crow and, in his jealousy, sent Artemis to kill Coronis (the crow, the bringer of the bad news has been black ever since). The unborn child Asclepius was snatched from her and given to the Centaur Chiron to rear. Asclepius's cult was widespread, each shrine having its own sacred snakes and baths. The main part of the ritual associated with Asclepius was to sleep in one of his temples and await a visitation from the god. His most important sanctuary was on the island of Cos where Hippocrates, the 'Father of Medicine', took over his work.

Athene The Greek goddess of war. She was a patron of arts and crafts and the personification of wisdom. Early legends say that she sprang fully armed from the forehead of Zeus. The Parthenon, in Athens, was built in her honour. In Homer she supports the Greeks against the Trojans and especially favours Odysseus throughout his wanderings.

Athene was the goddess of war but she took no real pleasure in battle even though she never lost. She invariably triumphed over Ares as she was far more intelligent and was a much greater strategist than him. She owned no weapons of her own but if they were needed she would borrow them from Zeus. Athene much preferred to settle disputes by arbitration than by violence and she was very liberal in her decisions, nearly always giving her casting vote to the accused in a close verdict.

Athene was as modest as Artemis but had a kinder disposition. When Teiresias, the Greek prophet, stumbled upon her in her bathroom and saw her naked she gently laid her hands over his eyes and though he was blinded she gave him the gift of inner sight. He became the greatest seer of his time and was featured in many Greek legends and stories.

A Centaur's Family *after the artist Sebastiano Ricci. They are shown in the woodland setting typical of Greek mythology.* Christie's Images

Once when she asked Hephaestus to make her some armour he refused payment and said he would do it as a labour of love. Athene misunderstood what he said and his motives so when she went to visit him in his smithy to see how he was getting on she was shocked by his behaviour. He thrust himself upon her in an attempt to violate her and when she pushed him away in disgust his seed fell upon the earth near Athens and fertilised mother earth. The product of this union was Erichthonius, a hideous child whose lower body represented a serpent. Earth was so disgusted by this child and the thought of Hephaestus's attempted rape of Athene that she would have nothing to do with it. The gentler Athene took it upon herself to look after the child and many thought that she was indeed his mother.

Atalanta See Meleager.

Atlas A Titan condemned to stand in the west holding up the sky as punishment for fighting with Cronus against Zeus.in the battle for Olympia. He was visited by Perseus during his journeys after cutting off Medusa's head, the sight of which turned him to stone, where-upon he became identified with Mount Atlas in North West Africa. His unique punishment gave the ancient Greeks an explanation as to why the sky did not fall.

Attis Originally an early vegetation god with a spring festival of death and resurrection which originated in Phrygia — Central Asia Minor. He was the consort of Cybele.

Bellerephon Many of the tales of Bellerophon are similar to those of

Heracles and Theseus and probably originated from primitive folk-lore before they became part of Greek legend. He is best known for his association with the fabulous winged horse Pegasus which helped him when he killed the Chimera and afterwards when he defeated the Amazons. Later Bellerophon made the mistake of flying to Olympus on Pegasus. Zeus was so outraged at this presumption of a mortal that he sent a gadfly which stung Pegasus under the tail whereupon he reared up and sent Bellerophon crashing to the earth. He spent the rest of his days wretched, lame and blind always shunning the company of other men.

Boreas Boreas is the north or north-east wind in Greece and like all winds sometimes depicted in the form of a horse.

Cadmus The son of the Phoenician king Agenor and the legendary founder of the city of Thebes. The Greeks believed it was Cadmus who had introduced their alphabet from the Phoenicians. According to legend he was told by the Oracle at Delphi to found a city where a cow lay down. He purchased a cow from some cowherds and followed it to the site of Thebes where it lay down with weariness beside a spring. Cadmus sacrificed the cow to Athene but when he went to the spring to cleanse himself he found it was guarded by a dragon which he killed. Athene appeared before him and told him to sew the dragons teeth in the ground. A crop of fully armed men sprang up and fought each other until only five were left. These five were said to be the ancestors of Theban nobility. Cadmus married Harmonia, the daughter of Ares and Aphrodite, and had several children including Semele the mother of Dionysus by Zeus.

Calypso Minor goddess, daughter of Atlas, living on the remote island of Orygia where she kept Odysseus for seven years until ordered by Zeus to send him home to Ithaca. She offered Odysseus eternal youth but he refused.

Cassandra She was one of the daughters of King Priam of Troy and regarded as the most beautiful. She was given the power of prophecy by Apollo, but was then doomed to be disbelieved because she refused him her love. Cassandra tried in vain to warn the Trojans about the wooden horse. After the sack of Troy she was brought home by Agamemnon and murdered along with him.

Castor and Pollux, Polydeuces The twin brothers of Helen and the sons of Leda. Among their many exploits they took part in the Argonauts' expedition. They carried off the daughters of a king of

Messina and when the girls' brothers fought to rescue them Castor was killed. Polydeuces pleaded with Zeus saying that he not want to live without his brother — it had been prophesied that only one son of Leda should die. Although Castor and Polydeuces were the twin sons of Leda they had different fathers. Castor's father was Tyndareus, a king of Sparta and a mortal, whereas Polydeuces was born of Zeus. Polydeuces was carried to Olympus where he refused immortality unless Castor could also share it. Zeus decided to allow them to spend alternative days in heaven and in the Underworld.and as a reward for their brotherly love set their image in the stars as twins.

A Roman bronze figure of three-headed Cerberus, the guardian dog of the Underworld. Christie's Images

Centaurs Centaurs were a tribe of wild creatures, half horse half human, living particularly in the wooded mountains of Thessaly. They are probably pre-Homeric, and for the Greeks they represented primitive desires and anti-social habits. They were always getting drunk, chasing women and fighting.

Cerberus Cerberus was the monstrous dog which guarded the entrance to the Underworld. In some stories he has 50 heads but is usually depicted as having three. He has to be retrieved from hell as one of Heracles' tasks (See Heracles).

Charon The ferry man of Greek mythology who takes the souls of the dead, in his boat, across the River Styx. He will only do this if the funeral rites have been properly performed and the fare, a small coin, is put in the mouth under the tongue of the corpse. Penniless souls were left in limbo on the banks of the Styx. On the other side of the river was the palace of Hades guarded by his three-headed dog Cerberus.

Charybdis A whirlpool in the Straits of Messina where the currents can be strong and dangerous. In the Odyssey Charybdis is placed opposite the monster Scylla when Odysseus is faced with a choice of two evils.

Chimera This was the fire breathing she-monster with a lion's head, goat's body and the tail of a serpent.which was killed by Bellerophon.

Chiron A son of Cronus and, unlike his fellow Centaurs, grows to become wise and kindly. He is the teacher of such heroes as Jason, Achilles and Asclepius. He was famous for his knowledge of archery, music and medicine. After being accidentally killed by Heracles he is put in the heavens as the constellation Sagittarius.

Cronos A Titan, the youngest son of Uranus (Heaven) and Ge (Earth).

Cybele The great mother-goddess of Phrygia where she was represented by a sacred stone and worshipped along with her youthful lover Attis. Cybele led a primitive cult which included purification by bathing in the blood of a sacrificed bull. A toned-down version of her ecstatic rites and ceremonies spread to Greece by the 5th century BC.

Demeter The Greek corn goddess associated with the ritual which celebrated the death and rebirth of the corn. Through the priestesses of Demeter brides and bridegrooms are blessed with fruitfulness. Although Demeter had no husband of her own, while still young she bore a daughter Core and a son Iacchus to Zeus.

Core was also recognised as Persephone, the queen of the Underworld. Hades, the god of the Underworld, had taken a fancy to Core on one of his lustful trips to the upper world so he went to Zeus to ask his permission to marry her. Zeus knew that Demeter would be heartbroken if Core was taken from her to live in the gloomy and lifeless world of Tartarus but he did not really want to upset his elder brother either. Instead of making any decision he told Hades that he could neither give nor refuse him permission to marry Core. Hades took this as a clear signal that he could do as he pleased without worrying about what Zeus had to say so, when he came across Core out picking flowers, he abducted her into his chariot and fled with her back to the Underworld. As Zeus had predicted Demeter was devastated by this abduction of her beloved daughter, she went about the earth forbidding any tree to bear fruit, any plant to flower or any crop to grow until the land was completely barren.

The pleas of mankind reached Olympus and all the gods begged Demeter to bring fruitfulness back to the earth but she was resolute, she wanted her daughter back. In the end Zeus was forced to send Hermes to Tartarus with a message for Hades begging him to release Core. A condition of being allowed to return from the Underworld was that no food of the dead had been consumed whilst there. Core had been so miserable in the land of gloom that she had not eaten a thing during her stay so Hades was obliged to send her back. As she was leaving Tartarus one of Hades' servants commented on the fact that he had seen her eat some pomegranate seeds so this would make it impossible for her to return to the upper world. When this news reached the utterly dejected Demeter she refused to go to Olympus or to lift the curse off the barren and desolate land.

A Parian marble group showing a youthful Dionysus with a satyr. Dionysus — Bacchus in Roman mythology — was an important god, beloved of cultists. It was as part of the spring festival of Great Dionysia that the great Athenian dramatists performed their plays. Christie's Images

In the end it took the pleading of Rhea, the mother of Zeus and Hades, to reach an equitable compromise. The deal was that Hades could have Core for three months of the year where she would assume the title of Persephone, queen of the Underworld, and that Demeter could have her for the other nine months.

Diomedes Diomedes was a Greek hero from Argos. He played a leading part in the Trojan War where his disciplined courage contrasted with the reckless Achilles. He wounded both Ares and Aphrodite, lead an attack on Troy in the absence of Achilles and raided the Trojan camp with Odysseus. He also helped Odysseus to steal the Palladium, the sacred image of Athene on which the fortunes of Troy depended.

Dionysus A Greek god associated with wine, the release of mass emotion and with a fertility cult. He was generally said to be the son of Zeus and Semele. He was taught the use of the vine and ivy, a mild intoxicant when chewed. He is a symbol of everlasting life and, on his triumphant return to Greece, was accepted by Apollo at Delphi where his cult continued there but in a less frenzied form.

When Dionysus was 'born for the second time' from the thigh of Zeus (See Zeus) Hera's jealousy once again showed itself, she instructed the Titans to boil him to death in a cauldron. He was rescued from this fate by Rhea who revived and revitalised him. To protect him from Hera's vengeance Hermes changed him into a ram and delivered him to some shepherds on Mount Nysa where he grew to manhood. It was during his time on Mount Nysa that he discovered the art of the vine and how to make wine. Hera now recognised who he was and drove him mad. In this state of madness he travelled all over Europe with his teacher Silenus and a wild army of satyrs taking his vine with him. This rather frightening image of Dionysus was probably rooted in pre Greek mythology.

When he eventually returned from Europe it was Rhea who once again came to his aid. She purified him of his madness and taught him the dark series of her cult, the Mysteries. Restored to sanity he travelled all over Greece and the Greek islands where his joyful behaviour tinged with the threat of menace soon established his deity. He arrived at Icaria where he needed to hire a ship to continue his travels. The ship he hired belonged to pirates who, having no idea who he was, planned to sail to Asia Minor to sell him as a slave. Once at sea Dionysus discovered their ulterior motive and wreaked his revenge upon them; he turned their oars into serpents, entwined their masts with his vine and filled their ship with monstrous beasts. He turned himself into a lion and chased the pirates overboard where they were changed into dolphins. When Dionysus came to the isle of Naxos he met and married Ariadne who had been deserted there by Theseus after his adventures on Crete. They then travelled to Argos where Perseus challenged him and it was only after Dionysus had killed a large number of his men that Perseus admitted his mistake and built a temple in his honour. With his deity now fully recognised throughout Greece Dionysus ascended to Olympus where he lived with the other gods.

Echo and Narcissus after Jean - Françoise Millet. Christie's Images

Echo and Narcissus Echo was a nymph deprived of normal speech by Hera so that she could only repeat the words of others. She fell in love with Narcissus, a beautiful boy and son of another nymph. Narcissus, however, was in love with his own reflection so he took no notice of Echo who, in her sadness, pined away leaving only her voice. Narcissus, gazing longingly at his reflection, also eventually pined away.

Eos A Greek goddess of the Dawn. There are many legends of the beautiful young men she carried off to be her lovers and it could be that such legends are a euphemism for death

Erechtheus Son of the Earth and often represented as a serpent below his waist (See Athene). He was worshipped with Athene on the Acropolis at Athens. The temple, known as the Erechtheum, contains a snake pit and the tomb of Cecrops, the mythical first king of Athens.

A Roman marble statuette of Cupid who was the Roman equivalent of the Eros, the Greek god of love. Christie's Images

Eros Greek god of Love generally said to be the son of Aphrodite. He is usually depicted as a playful character carrying a bow and arrow — though he does have a cruel side to him.

The Furies or Erinnyes These were Greek spirits of vengeance who specialised in the punishment of wrongdoings within the family — particularly of murder. The Furies were represented as old women with dog's heads and writhing serpents for hair. They could be personified as pangs of conscience and their victims died in torment.

Eurydice See Orpheus.

Galatea A sea-nymph whom Polyphemus, the Cyclops, fell madly in love with. She rejected his attentions as she loved a shepherd called Acis. In his rage Polyphemus crushed Acis under a huge rock but the triumphant Galatea caused a spring

The Rape of Ganymede *after Sir Peter Paul Rubens. In later Greek legend Zeus, attracted by the beauty of Ganymede, abducts him in the form of an eagle.* Christie's Images

to flow from under the rock and Acis became god of the stream.

Ganymede A Trojan prince who was carried off by the gods to serve as a cup bearer to Zeus.

Graces The Three Graces (or Charities) Aglaia, Euphrosyne and Thalia are daughters of Zeus and personify beauty, charm and grace. They are often seen attendant on Aphrodite.

Hades One of the three sons of the Titan Cronus and brother to Zeus and Poseidon. He was the husband of Persephone and ruler of the Underworld. In Greek mythology the dead are said to go to the 'House of Hades' and no favours were expected of him and no temples dedicated. Hades seldom leaves the Underworld and rarely allows any of his subjects to do so. There were some who tried but very few lived to tell the tale and so descriptions of the Underworld, Tartarus, were very sparse and sketchy.

Hades' knowledge of what goes on upon the earth is also very limited as he really only ventures there when his lust gets the better of him over a particular mortal maiden he might fancy. His most prized possession is the helmet of invisibility made for him by Zeus's armourers the Cyclopes. They gave it to him as a reward for his rescuing and releasing them from Tartarus. Hades has no material possessions above ground, but all the earth's precious gems and minerals buried in the ground belong to him

Harpies Harpies were originally wind spirits but later they became winged monsters who snatched away food or carried people off to their deaths. In the story of the Argonauts they torment the blind seer Phineus (See Golden Fleece). They are sometimes portrayed as birds with women's faces.

Hebe The personification of youth, although a minor deity said to be the daughter of Zeus and Hera. She is the server of Nectar to the Olympian gods and is sometimes the wife of Heracles after his deification.

Hecate A primitive pre-Greek goddess of the Underworld who later came to be associated with Artemis.

Helios A Titan, a Greek sun god generally thought of as driving his chariot east to west across the sky. In later legend he is associated with Apollo or Hyperion.

Hephaestus The son of Zeus and Hera who were themselves brother and sister. Hephaestus was such an ugly and ill tempered little child that Hera was disgraced and embarrassed by him to the extent that she hurled him down from Mount Olympus in disgust. Hephaestus escaped injury because he fell into the sea where he was found by the gentle Nymphs Thetis and Eurynome who took him to their underwater caves where they tended and looked after him. Hephaestus had been a smithy to the gods of Olympus and he set up a workshop in the nymphs' grotto where he made all manner of beautiful brooches and ornaments for them as a means of repaying their kindness to him.

Sometime later Hera met Thetis and, noticing her stunning adornments, asked her where she had got such wonderful jewellery. When she was told that it was the work of Hephaestus she immediately asked him to return to Olympus with her where she set him up in a most magnificent smithy. The reconciliation of Hera with her once most despised son became so complete that Hephaestus even had the courage to question Zeus about his abhorrent treatment of Hera. He strongly criticised Zeus for having suspended his mother from the heavens after her attempted rebellion. This harsh criticism from his child was more than Zeus could bear and, for a second time, Hephaestus was hurled from Olympus. This time Hephaestus was not so lucky, he spent a whole day falling eventually crashing to earth on the island of Lemnos and breaking both his legs.

Although he was a god and therefore immortal his body was badly broken and he was in a pitiful state when he was found by some shepherds. They looked after him until he was, in time, pardoned and brought back to Olympus where he could only get about with the aid of some golden leg supports which he made for himself.

Hera The wife and also the sister of Zeus as both were children of Cronus. She is generally portrayed as being violently jealous of the many love affairs of Zeus and cruel to her rivals. In Homer she is hostile to Troy but in the Argonaut legend she is Jason's guide and support.

Heracles One of the greatest of all Greek heroes, the son of Zeus and a mortal princess called Alcmene. All his famous exploits derive from his strength and courage. When Hera, as usual jealous and angry, heard about his birth she sent two snakes to kill him. Heracles was still in his cradle but was already so strong that he strangled the snakes with his bare hands. He grew up to be a mighty warrior but Hera still hated him. She caused him to be seized by a fit of madness whereupon he killed his wife and children. He invoked the gods pleading with them for a way to be purified from these awful deeds.

He was advised to go and serve a Mycenaean king called Eurystheus for 12 years and to perform whatever Labours might be set for him. Heracles was mortified at the thought of serving a man he knew to be far inferior to himself yet, afraid of his father Zeus, he placed himself at Eurystheus's disposal.

There are stories which describe the many strange and wonderful weapons used by Heracles given to him by the gods, but his main weapon was his trusty club hewn by his own hand from the wild olive. His nephew Iolaus often shared in his Labours both as compatriot and serving as his charioteer. (See main stories, p26 etc.)

Hermaphroditos Son of Hermes and Aphrodite. When he refused the advances of the nymph Salmacis the gods answered her prayer that their bodies could be joined as one. This is an example of an aetiological myth which was used to explain the existence of bisexuals.

Hermes The messenger god. It is generally accepted that Hermes

A bronze Hellenistic figure of Heracles.
Christie's Images

was the son of Zeus and Maia, daughter of Atlas. He was known for his childish tricks and ingenuity. He invented the lyre by stringing a tortoiseshell with cow gut and is recognised as the patron of all wayfarers, traders, travellers and thieves.

One of the best known stories about Hermes was his theft of Apollo's cattle. When Apollo discovered the loss he went in search of Hermes. He tracked him down to a cave where he discovered that he had constructed an inventive musical instrument out of cow-gut stretched across a tortoiseshell. When Apollo, wondering where Hermes had acquired the cow-gut, noticed two hides outside the cave he picked him up and carried him to Olympus where he took him before Zeus and charged him with theft of his cattle. Zeus didn't really want to believe that his mischievous but likable youngest son was a thief but Apollo persisted and eventually Hermes owned up. Hermes gave Apollo back his herd claiming that he had only slaughtered two which he had cut up and offered as a sacrifice to the gods. After what was the first animal sacrifice ever made Hermes declared that he had only eaten his portion and burned the rest.

Despite himself, Apollo was very impressed with the musical lyre Hermes had created and readily made a deal with him. Much to the amusement of Zeus he agreed to swap his cattle for the instrument. Zeus, in turn impressed with the ingenuity of Hermes, made him his herald and gave him a staff of authority, a round hat for protection against the elements, and winged sandals to carry him with the swiftness of the wind

Hestia It is to Hestia's credit that she never takes part in wars or disputes. This put her morally above the other great Olympians and she was widely worshipped for her humanity and for being the most benign of the gods. After the battle against the Titans and the ursurption of Cronus she was courted by both Apollo and Poseidon but she had taken an oath that she would remain a virgin. Zeus saw that this avoided any possible damaging conflict on Olympus and accordingly rewarded her by offering her the first victim of any mortal sacrifice. She was worshipped in the home as goddess of the Hearth and most households would have had a small shrine to her.

Horae 'The Hours' were originally the Greek goddesses of the Seasons and were three in number indicating the growth, flowering and ripening of vegetation. They are sometimes associated with the Three Graces.

Hyperion A Titan, a sun god and the father of Dawn (Eos), Sun (Helios) and Moon (Selene).

Hypnos The Greek god of sleep, son of Night and the brother of Death. He is generally thought of as a winged boy who touches the foreheads of the weary or pours a sleeping draught from a cup. In the Iliad he carries the dead warriors from the battlefield.

Icarus Son of the inventor Daedalus, who offended Minos the king of Crete. They escaped together by means of artificial wings fastened by wax. Unheeding of his father's warnings, Icarus flew too close to the sun which melted the wax and caused him to fall to a watery grave.

Io She was a priestess of Hera at Argos and a lover of Zeus who turned her into a heifer to protect her from the jealous Hera. Hera was not deceived and set the giant Argus to watch her. Hera then sent a gadfly which drove Io all over Europe and Egypt where she was eventually restored by Zeus.

Iris The Greek goddess of the rainbow and messenger of the gods, perhaps because a rainbow links the sky and earth.

Laomedon The king of Troy and father of Priam, noted for his treachery. He refused payment to Apollo and Poseidon when they built his city walls so they sent a sea monster which would have devoured his daughter Hesione had not Heracles intervened. Laomedon had promised his famous horses to Heracles for rescuing

The Fall of Icarus *by the artist Ryckaert.* Christie's Images

his daughter but again did not keep his part of the deal. The horses in question were the ones Zeus had given to Troy in return for a Trojan prince called Gannymede who was carried off to be his cup bearer. When Laomedon refused to give up the horses Heracles sacked the city and killed all of Laomedon's sons except Priam.

Laestrygones   These are a race of cannibal giants who, in the Odyssey, sink all but one of Odysseus's ships.

Lapiths   A primitive mountain tribe in Thessaly related to the Centaurs through common descent from Ixion. Ixion was a king of the Lapiths and, according to legend, the first man to kill a blood relative. For this he was purified by Zeus but, later, he tried to rape Hera. He was deceived by a cloud made in her image on which he begat the father of the Centaurs. As a punishment for his sins Ixion was fixed to a revolving wheel in hell to suffer for eternity. Lapiths are chiefly famous for their battle with the drunken Centaurs at the marriage of their king Pirithous.

Leda   An Aetolian princess, the wife of Tyndareus — King of Sparta — the mother of Clytemnestra, Helen, Castor and Polydeuces (Pollux). Leda was loved by Zeus who came to her in the form of a swan. She gave birth to an egg from which were hatched Helen and Polydeuces, while Castor and Clytemnestra were fathered by Tyndareus.

Leto   A Titan, the mother of Apollo and Artemis by Zeus.

Medea   The daughter of Aeëtes, king of Colchis, a priestess of Hecate and a witch. She helped Jason win the Golden Fleece (See Golden Fleece). Jason and Medea went to Corinth where he abandoned her for the king's daughter. In revenge Medea destroyed the girl and her father, killed her two children then escaped in a dragon-drawn chariot, first to Athens, then to Asia.

Meleager   The son of Oeneas, King of Calydon, and Althea (in some stories his father was Ares). When Meleager was still a baby it was fated that he could only continue to live so long as a certain brand on the hearth remained unburnt. His mother hid this brand to ensure that her son would live.

Meleager grew up to be the best javelin thrower in Greece and, along with almost every other hero in Greek mythology according to whose stories were told, was one of the Argonauts. Oeneas incurred the wrath of Artemis when, one year, he forgot to include her in his sacrifices to the gods. In revenge she sent a huge and ferocious boar to roam and ravage the countryside of Calydon. The king called upon all the great fighters and heroes of Greece to help him rid the land of this beast promising that whoever killed it could have its pelt and tusks as a trophy.

Amongst the heroic hunters who turned up was Atalanta, a girl who had been rejected at birth by her father in disappointment at not having a male heir. Atalanta had been abandoned in the mountains where she had been suckled by a bear sent by Artemis to help her. She grew up amongst a clan of hunters who had found her and, like Artemis, had remained a virgin and always carried arms. Several of the male hunting party made comments about hunting with a woman and would have refused to have her with them had not Meleager, who had fallen in love with Atalanta, threatened to abandon the hunt. The four most outspoken critics of the huntress were Meleager's uncles, the brothers of Althea, so the hunt began under very bad auspices in which Artemis had played no little part.

It was a chaotic affair with so many people charging about shouting and yelling trying to flush the boar out, but the first blood was drawn by Atalanta. Two centaurs involved in the chase tried to ravish and violate her so she shot and killed them with her arrows. At the scent of blood the boar came crashing out of the undergrowth killing and maiming several members of the party and in the ensuing commotion some were even killed by other hunters. Atalanta let fly with an arrow which pierced the boar behind its ear and, when it flew at Theseus in pain and rage, Meleager dispatched it with one thrust of his spear.

Meleager flayed the beast and handed the pelt to Atalanta saying that she was the one who had drawn the first blood. Meleager's eldest uncle was furious; he said that if Meleager who had actually killed the boar did not want the trophy, it should go to the worthiest and bravest fighter there — namely himself. Meleager was furious and when his youngest uncle sided with his brother he killed them both. The two remaining uncles now declared war on Meleager and in the battles that followed they too were killed. The Furies, the avengers of murders in the family, instructed Althea that she must put the untouched fire brand on the hearth and when she did so the searing burning pain Meleager felt so weakened him that he was easily overrun by his enemies. In her grief Althea committed suicide.

After the boar hunt and, as a result of the courage of his daughter, Atalanta's father now gladly recognised her and welcomed her home. He was still eager to have a male heir to succeed him and instructed her to prepare to take a husband. Atalanta agreed on the condition that any successful suitor must be able to beat her in a foot race and if he failed she should be allowed to take his life. As she was the swiftest mortal alive many an unfortunate young prince made a premature journey to Tartarus, until an Arcadian prince by the name of Melanion invoked the aid of Aphrodite. The goddess of love was not enamoured by virgins so she agreed to help Melanion. She gave him three golden apples and told him to drop them strategically during the race. As he dropped the apples Atalanta stooped to pick them up and this slowed her sufficiently for him to pass the winning tape just in front of her.

The marriage took place at a temple of Zeus but Melanion could not wait to get home and persuaded Atalanta to lie with him there. Zeus was outraged at this violation of his sacred place and changed them both into lions. The Greeks believed that lions did not mate with lions but only with leopards and so in this way Melanion and Atalanta were never allowed to consummate their marriage. Aphrodite fully sanctioned this punishment as she was displeased with Melanion over his lack of gratitude for the golden apples and wasn't impressed with Atalanta's desire to remain a virgin.

This painting by Nicolas Poussin shows King Midas bathing at the source of the river Pactolus in an attempt to rid himself of the 'golden touch'.
Christie's Images

Midas A king of Phrygia about whom many legends were told. He once entertained Silenus who had been left behind drunk after one of Dionysus's wild parties. As a reward for his hospitality Dionysus granted Midas's wish that everything he touched should be turned to gold. The novelty of this gift soon wore off as not only stones, flowers and the furnishings of his house turned to gold as Midas touched them but also anything he ate or drunk. Dionysus told him he would get rid of the golden touch if he went to the source of the River Pactolus and bathed in it. The sands of the Pactolus have been golden ever since.

Midas also voted against Apollo in the famous musical contest he had with Pan. Apollo punished him with a pair of ass's ears, which only his barber knew about and, although having sworn to secrecy on the pain of death, the barber couldn't keep it to himself. He dug a hole in the ground and whispered the secret to the earth. Where he had dug the hole some reeds grew up and, as the wind rustled them, they disclosed the truth about Midas's affliction. On hearing that his disgrace had become public knowledge Midas condemned the barber to death and he, himself, perished miserably.

Minotaur A monster with a bull's head and a human body. When Minos overthrew his brothers and took the throne of Crete he boasted that the gods would answer any prayer he offered as proof of his right to reign. To verify this claim he set up an altar to Poseidon and invoked the god, asking him to deliver a bull for sacrifice. A pure white bull emerged from the sea and its beauty was such that Minos could not bring himself to slaughter it. He placed it amongst his herds in the field and sacrificed another beast instead. Poseidon was mightily aggrieved at this affront so made Minos's wife Pasiphaë fall in love with the white bull.

Pasiphaë told a local carpenter called Daedalus about her strange obsession and he promised to help her. He constructed a hollow wooden cow big enough to hold Pasiphaë and took it to the meadow where the white bull was grazing. Having helped Pasiphaë climb into the contraption, with her legs pushed down inside the cow's hindquarters, he retired. The bull mounted the wooden cow, satisfying Pasiphaë's desires and she later gave birth to the Minotaur. When King Minos consulted an oracle to find out the best way to hide Pasiphaë's disgrace he was told to get the craftsman Daedalus to build him the inextricable maze called the Labyrinth at Knossos. Minos spent the rest of his life there where he concealed Pasiphaë and the Minotaur, at the heart of the maze, until Theseus killed it.

Morpheus One of the sons of Hypnos, he sends dreams and visions.

Muses These are the nine daughters of Zeus and the Titan Mnemosyne (Memory): Clio, Euterpe, Thalia, Melpomene, Terpsichore, Erato, Polyhymnia, Urania and Calliope. They are said to give the gift of art, knowledge and song but seldom without cost. The Muses judged the contest between Apollo and Marsyas the satyr who presumed to challenge Apollo in a flute playing contest. When Apollo won he had Marsyas tied to a tree and flayed alive. All the nymphs and creatures of the woods wept for him and their tears became the River Meander. Each of the Muses presides over a branch of the arts or sciences and as embodiments of the highest artistic benefits to man they are presided over by Apollo.

A detail of winged Nike from Ephesus.
Life-File/Andrew Ward

Nemesis Goddess of retribution.

Nereus A primitive sea god said to be endowed with wisdom and the gift of prophecy. He is the father of the Nereids, sea nymphs, the most famous being Amphitrite — wife of Poseidon — and Thetis, the mother of Achilles.

Nessus The Centaur who assaulted Deianira, the wife of Heracles, and was subsequently killed by him. The blood which soaked Nessus's garment was later to kill Heracles and 'a shirt of Nessus' became proverbial for a fatal gift.

Oedipus The story of Oedipus is one of the most tragic of all the Greek legends. He was born the son of Lauis and Jocasta, the king and queen of Thebes. Before his birth Apollo had prophesied that one day he would kill his father so Lauis had him taken to the hills where, with a spike put through his feet, he was left to die. He was found by some herdsmen who taking pity on him took him to the court of King Polybus in Corinth. One day, after being ridiculed about his true parentage, he begged Polybus to tell him the truth about his birth but the king refused so he went to the oracle at Delphi. There he was told that it had been prophesied that one day he would kill his father and marry his mother so, in great distress he vowed never to return to Corinth.

His wanderings took him to Thebes where, quite by chance, he encountered Lauis who was riding in his chariot. The Theban king ordered Oedipus off the road telling him to make way for his betters and when the youth refused, a furious argument broke out. Lauis tried to drive his chariot over Oedipus but he got caught in the reins of his horses when Oedipus lunged at him and was dragged to his death. Oedipus had no idea who Lauis was, least of all that he was his father.

On arriving at Thebes Oedipus discovered that the city was being threatened by the Sphinx, a beast half woman-half lion, who killed any passersby who could not answer its riddle. The riddle was 'What is it that walks on four feet in the morning, two at noon and three in the evening'? Oedipus went to meet the Sphinx and said 'Man is the answer; he crawls on four feet as a baby, upright on two as a man and with the aid of a stick when old'. On being given the correct answer the Sphinx killed itself.

The Thebans were overjoyed and offered Oedipus their kingdom along with Jocasta, the widow of Lauis, to be his wife and queen. Still not knowing their true identities the two of them lived happily for many years and had four children until a plague came upon the land. A messenger was sent to the Delphic oracle to find out what caused the plague and what could be done about it. In all the ensuing investigations and questions that were asked Oedipus finally discovered the awful truth about himself and in his horror blinded himself. He wandered around Greece for the rest of his years in abject misery as a blind beggar with only his daughter Antigone for company.

Orpheus The son of Apollo and the muse Calliope, who played the lyre so beautifully that all the animals in the forest gathered round to hear him. Even the trees and the rocks were said to have been

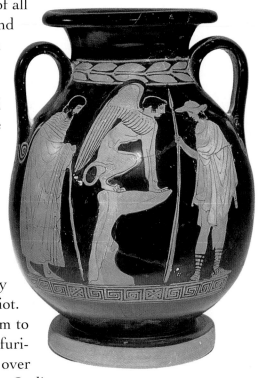

An Attic red-figure amphora showing Oedipus solving the riddle of the Sphinx. Red-figurework came in around 540BC; the figures are reserved in the colour of the red clay and the background is painted black. This means that the details on the figure can be painted rather than incised. Christie's Images

Orpheus playing his lyre to the animals of the forest after the artist Roelandt Savery (1576-1639).
Christie's Images

enchanted by his music. Orpheus sailed to Clochis with the Argonauts, his music helping them to overcome many of their difficulties.

Orpheus was married to the nymph Eurydice who trod on a snake one day whilst they were out in the woods, the poison from the serpent proved fatal and her soul was taken down to Tartarus. Orpheus went in search of his beloved nymph and followed her down to the Underworld. He begged Hades to release Eurydice and played his lyre for the king of Tartarus and his queen Persephone. The music was so beautiful that not only the king and the queen were moved but all of Hades's subjects forgot their eternal torments and wept for him. In wonderment Hades made a very rare decision to let one of his subjects go. He said that Eurydice could follow Orpheus back to the upper air on the condition that Orpheus did not look back for her until they reached the mortal world. When Orpheus saw the daylight he looked back to make sure Eurydice was following him and in an instant she vanished back to the Underworld. In his despair Orpheus sat in the woods playing his lyre and singing of his grief. The women worshippers of Dionysus attended him but he so despised their love that eventually, in frustration, they tore him to pieces. The Muses buried his body where it is said a nightingale continuously sings over his grave. His lyre was placed in the heavens as a constellation.

Pan Pan is generally represented as having goat's ears, horns and legs. He was a fertility god and could be dangerous especially if disturbed in the heat of the day when he was asleep.

The origin of Pan is somewhat confused. and he probably derived from a more primitive culture than the Greek one which had him as the son of Hermes. According to this myth Hermes fathered him to a nymph who was so terrified at the sight of him at birth that she ran away. Hermes kept him on Olympus for the amusement of the other gods who exploited his easy-going nature. Apollo learned the art of prophesy from him whilst Hermes discovered how to make the Pan pipes which, incidentally, he claimed as his own invention and sold to Apollo as such.

Pan and Syrinx after Willem de Heusch. Christie's Images

In later mythology Pan was a lustful fun-loving god who lived in Arcadia with the wood nymphs and shepherds. They spent most of their time in this rustic idyll in revelry and tending to the herds of goats and sheep. Pan was generally a lazy character although he was a patron of hunters and would often help them in their pursuits. He liked nothing better than his afternoon sleeps after a night of lustful revelry and would frighten the life out of anyone who woke him with a terrible roar. Included amongst his many amorous conquests were the nymph Syrinx and the goddess Selene. His seduction of the chaste Syrinx was the origin of his famous Pan pipes; he chased her to the banks of the River Ladon where she pleaded with mother earth to disguise her as a reed, Pan could not distinguish her from all the other reeds so he cut several stems which, together, formed his famous pipes. In his seduction of Semele he disguised his hairy black body with a beautiful white fleece, Selene was so enamoured by this that she rode upon his back and was quite happy to let him do as he pleased with her not realising who he really was.

Pegasus A fabulous winged horse which was said to have sprung from the body of Medusa after Perseus had beheaded her.

Peleus Involved in many of the great heroic stories including the Calydonian Boar Hunt, the battle between the Lapiths and the Centaurs and the voyage of the Argonauts. He is probably best remembered for his marriage to Thetis by whom he fathered Achilles. Peleus first met Thetis and her sisters, the Nereids, when he was returning home on the Argo. It was at his wedding that the uninvited Eris threw down the fateful apple that led to the Judgment of Paris and the Trojan War.

The head of Orpheus in the fine white marble of the Aegean island of Paros. Parian marble was later to give its name to the look-alike porcelain invented by W. T. Copeland in 1842 for the purpose of making statuary. It was used extensively by Copeland, Minton and Wedgwood. Christie's Images

Perseus His best known stories concern the Gorgon Medusa and the rescue of Andromeda. Perseus was the son of Zeus and Danae who was the daughter of Acrisius, king of Argos. Acrisius imprisoned Danae in a dungeon because an oracle had told him that his grandson would one day kill him. He reasoned that if he imprisoned Danae no one would come near her and she could not possibly conceive a son. However Zeus had taken a fancy to the beautiful young princess and came to her prison in a shower of gold as a result of which she bore him a son, Perseus. Although the king did not believe that Zeus was the father, Perseus he did not dare murder his own daughter and grandchild, so he locked them in a wooden chest and cast them into the sea. They were rescued by a fisherman off the island of Seriphos and protected by its king Polydectes. As Perseus grew to manhood he had to protect his mother against Polydectes who tried to force marriage upon her. One day Polydectes gathered his friends and pretended he was going to ask for the hand of a princess in marriage and asked them all for a wedding gift. Perseus, delighted that Polydectes was not going to marry his mother, expressed his regrets at having no suitable gift or the gold to buy one but rashly stated that he would contrive to win whatever gift Polydectes might name. He would even bring him the head of the Gorgon Medusa if that was his desire. Polydectes, seeing a way to be rid of Perseus, told him that would

Polyphemus and Galatea *after the artist Luca Giordano. The sea-nymph Galatea is shown rejecting the advances of the Cyclops Polyphemus.* Christie's Images

please him more than any gift in the world. The head of the Gorgon Medusa, with its serpents for hair, was so grotesque that anyone who gazed upon it would instantly be petrified with fright.

The Gorgons were three immortal sisters, Medusa, Stheno and Euryale. Athene came to the aid of Perseus by showing him images of all three sisters to enable him to distinguish Medusa.and she warned him never to look at Medusa directly. She gave him a brightly polished shield so that he could look at a reflection of Medusa and not at the Gorgon herself. Hermes also helped Perseus by giving him a sickle to cut off the Gorgon's head. Before he could complete his task Perseus still needed a pair of winged sandals, a magic sack to contain the decapitated head, and Hades's much prized helmet of invisibility. The whereabouts of these items were known only to the Graeae, sisters of the Gorgons.

The Graeae had only one tooth and a single eye which they shared between the three of them. As they were passing them to each other Perseus crept up behind them and snatched the eye and the tooth and would not return them until he was given the information he needed. Perseus collected the magic sack and the helmet then, donning the winged sandals, flew to the Gorgons lair where he found them asleep. Averting his eyes from Medusa he gazed at her reflection in his shield and cut off her head with the sickle. He put the head in the sack and donning the helmet, to make himself invisible, escaped from the remaining Gorgons.

At sunset Perseus arrived at the palace of the Titan Atlas in the west where the hospitality he was shown was so poor that he showed Medusa's head to Atlas. The legend has it that Atlas was immediately turned to stone — thus creating Mount Atlas. Continuing on his journey Perseus caught sight of a beautiful girl chained naked to a rock.whom he fell immediately in love with. This was Andromeda whose mother had angered Poseidon by boasting that her daughter was more beautiful than the Nereids. In his anger, Poseidon had sent a sea monster to destroy the land. This monster could only be placated by the sacrifice of Andromeda and hence she was chained to a rock to await it. As the sea monster approached Andromeda Perseus took to the air and beheaded it with his sickle.

Perseus returned to the island of Seriphos with Andromeda, who he had now married, to find his mother, threatened by the violence of Polydectes, taking refuge in a temple. He went straight to the palace of Polydectes and produced the promised wedding gift, the sight of which turned Polydectes immediately to stone. He gave the head of Medusa to Athene, who fixed it on her shield, and the winged sandals, the magic sack and helmet to Hermes who returned them to their rightful owners.

Phoebe In early Greek legend, the daughter of Uranus (Heaven) and Ge (Earth) and the mother of Leto. She was later identified with Artemis.

Philoctetes One of the Greek leaders in the Trojan War who had to be left behind on the island of Lemnos suffering from a snake bite. Odysseus, who had heard that Troy could not be taken without Philoctetes, went to Lemnos, with Diomedes, to fetch him (in some stories it is Neoptolemus, the son of Achilles, who goes with Odysseus). Philoctetes is reluctant to go knowing that they only want him for Heracles's bow and arrows which had been given to him for lighting the funeral pyre of Heracles. He would not have gone had it not been for the divine intervention of Heracles.

Phrixus and Helle Brother and sister, children of Athamas king of Aeolia and victims of their stepmother Ino's jealousy. They were about to be sacrificed in some primitive fertility rite, but escaped on the back of a golden ram sent by Zeus. Helle fell off into the sea but Phrixus made it to Colchis where he sacrificed the ram to Zeus — it became the constellation Aries. The Ram's golden fleece became famous when it was sought by Jason and the Argonauts.

Polyphemus One of the Cyclopes, who captures Odysseus and his men, shuts them up in a cave, and eats two of them every morning. They escape by blinding him in his one eye then slipping out with the sheep and goats the next morning. He is the son of Poseidon, and in answer to his cry for help, Poseidon delays Odysseus's return home (See Odysseus). Polyphemus's home has been placed by ancient tradition in eastern Sicily where there are the seven 'Scogli de Cyclopi', the rocks Polyphemus hurled after Odysseus as he escaped in his boat.

Poseidon The Greek god of earthquakes and later the sea and is worshipped with horses. He is said to have been the father of the horse Pegasus by the Gorgon Medusa. Poseidon has power over the sea and at the approach of his chariot storms will instantly abate. In Olympian mythology he is the son of Cronus and a brother to Zeus and Hades with the sea as his domain. He is particularly important to Athens as he was the father of the Athenian hero Theseus and competed for Attica with Athene (See Athene). In the Homeric poems he is the enemy of the Trojans because he was cheated when he and Apollo built the walls of Troy for Laomedon (when Zeus sent them there as a punishment for rebelling against him).

After the defeat of Cronus and the Titans the three brothers,

Sunset over the Temple of Poseidon on the Athens' Acropolis.
Life-File/Jeremy Hoare

Zeus, Hades and Poseidon, decided to draw lots to see who would rule the three kingdoms of heaven, the Underworld and the sea. Earth would be a common domain. As a result of the draw, Zeus won the heavens, Hades the Underworld and Poseidon the sea. Poseidon soon got greedy and cast his eyes on earthly possessions. In an attempt to claim Attica he went to the Acropolis at Athens and thrust his trident into the ground; sea water gushed out of the well he created which can still be seen today. Athene, however, had her own claim to Attica and challenged Poseidon. She planted the very first olive tree beside the well as a token of her stake. Poseidon was infuriated and challenged Athene to single armed combat but Zeus insisted that the dispute should go to arbitration amongst the Olympians. All the goddesses supported Athene's claim while the gods backed Poseidon. As Zeus was not really interested and did not vote, Athene won the arbitration by a majority of one.

Poseidon claims to have invented the horse but there is not much credence to this. He is, however worshipped and associated with horses. In his stables under the sea he has a great golden chariot which is drawn by a team of white horses.

Priam Priam was the son of Laomedon and the last king of Troy. He was said to have had many children, 50 sons and 50 daughters, by his wife and many concubines. In the Iliad he is already an old man, tired and exhausted by the sufferings of war, but he shows great tenderness and care to Helen. In later legends he was killed by Achilles's son Neoptolemus at the altar of Zeus.

An Attic red figure calyx crater showing Dionysus with cavorting satyrs. The calyx craters were used for wine-mixing.
Christie's Images

Satyrs In early mythology satyrs are half-bestial spirits of the woods and hills. They are mischievous and amorous and they often appear chasing nymphs or revelling with Dionysus at his drinking parties. In later mythology, in Hellenistic Arcadia, their more sinister aspect is forgotten.

Scylla Scylla is a sea monster in the Straits of Messina opposite Charybdis the whirlpool, past which Odysseus and the Argonauts had to sail. She was said to have had six heads and a ring of barking dogs round her belly. She was once a sea nymph but was changed into a sea monster by Circe.

Selene Pre-Greek or Eastern goddess of the Moon. Like Phoebe she is identified by the Greeks with Artemis. She was given horses to drive across the sky.

Semele The daughter of Cadmus, king of Thebes, and the mother of the god Dionysus by Zeus. After being persuaded by the jealous Hera to ask Zeus to appear to her in his true form she denied him entry to her bed, when he was refused he killed her with his thunderbolt. The unborn child Dionysus was taken from her body to be brought up by nymphs.

Silenus Originally a satyr but later depicted as a bearded man with horse's ears and is said to have been the tutor of Dionysus. He possesses special knowledge and wisdom which is inspired by wine drinking and he is generally depicted as being drunk.

Sphinx The Sphinx was a fabulous monster with a human head and the body of a lion. She originated in Egypt and came to Greece via the near East. In particular she is mentioned in Theban legends involving the House of Oedipus. (See Oedipus).

Styx The Styx is the river of the Underworld over which the souls of the dead are traditionally ferried by Charon. Achilles was dipped into it to make him invulnerable. One legend purports that Alexander the Great was killed by water from the Styx sent to him in a mule's hoof

Theseus Theseus, the son of Aegeus king of Athens, and thought to have been a contemporary of Heracles with whom he shares a number of similar exploits. As king, after the death of his father, he was said to have brought the Attic communities under the rule of Athens. He has a part in nearly every famous legend and is probably best known for killing the Minotaur. Every ninth year Athens had to send a tribute to King Minos on the island of Crete. This tribute was for the Athenians' murder of Minos's son Androgeus and consisted of seven youths and seven maidens who were sacrificed to the Minotaur to devour. The Minotaur was the bull-headed monster which Pasiphae, the wife of King Minos of Crete, had borne. The Minotaur lived in the Labyrinth, a maze so full of turnings and passages that, once inside, it was impossible to find a way out.

Theseus was to go with the next sacrifice in order to kill the Minotaur. On the two previous occasions, the ship which conveyed the 14 victims had carried black sails, but Theseus was confident that the gods were on his side, and Aegeus therefore gave him a white sail to hoist on return to show he had been successful. When they arrived in Crete, the daughter of Minos, Ariadne, saw Theseus and fell in love with him. She gave him a long thread to unwind as he searched the labyrinth for the Minotaur. Thus, when he found the

An Attic black figure amphora depicting Theseus slaying the Minotaur.

Minotaur and killed it, he was able to find his way out of the maze by following the thread. With the Minotaur dead, and having escaped the Labyrinth, the Athenians sailed for home. Theseus, however, forgot to change the sail from black to white and on seeing the black sail king Aegeus, thinking his son dead, threw himself into the sea. The sea was thus named the Aegean Sea. Theseus now became the king of Athens. In a later adventure he tried to capture the wife of Hades who caught him and imprisoned him until Heracles came to his rescue. He had been away from Athens for so long that the Athenians refused to have him back. He went to the island of Scyros where he died.

Thetis Chief of the Nereids, whom it was prophesied would bear a son mightier than his father. Because of this Zeus and Poseidon decided to marry her to a mortal, Peleus. Their son was Achilles. In the *Iliad* Thetis is humanised as a mother whose only concern is her son, and she is always aware that he is doomed to die young.

Titans Name for the earliest Greek gods, the children of the sky god Uranus and the earth goddess Ge. They feature heavily in the mythology of Greece.

Tyche A daughter of Zeus to whom he gave the power to decide the fortune of a mortal. She is totally arbitrary as to whether she gives or deprives and is represented juggling a ball to illustrate the uncertainty of chance. Anyone who brags about his riches or doesn't appreciate them will gain the wrath of Nemesis, the goddess of retribution, who humiliate the offender.

Zephyrus The west wind in Greek mythology and, like all winds, originally imagined in horse form. In the Iliad he is the father of Xanthus and Balius, the wonderful talking horses of Achilles which had been a wedding present from Poseidon to Peleus. He is sometimes thought of as the husband of Iris (the rainbow) and is also said to have deflected the discus which killed the youth Hyacinthus.

Zeus The father of gods and men. His usurpation of Cronus and his battle against the Titans represents the triumph of the Olympians over the pre-Greek deities. His authority is based on power and not morality. As well as all his legitimate children on Olympus, Athene, Apollo, Artemis and Ares, he has many other loves and children. In classical times Zeus became the supreme civic god and protector of law and justice.

Zeus's power derived from the powerful thunderbolts made for him by his armourers the Cyclopes. It was the dread of this fatal weapon which gave him the necessary control over the other gods and goddesses on Olympus. He had a long series of lustful adventures. He fathered children to three of the Titanesses; with Themis (Righteousness) he fathered the Horae — the Three Fates; with Eurynome he fathered the Charities and with Mnemosyne the Muses. He also fathered Persephone, the queen of the Underworld and the wife of his brother Hades, with the Nymph Styx. It was through these carnal liaisons that Zeus retained great power below the earth as well as on it and above it.

Amorous Zeus lay with numerous nymphs descended from the Titans or the gods and, after the creation of man, with mortals as well. No less than four great Olympian deities were born to him out of wedlock. First he fathered Hermes with Maia (daughter of Atlas and one of the Pleiades), next Apollo and Artemis with Leto (daughter of the Titans Coeus and Phoebe).

When the jealous Hera heard that Leto was carrying Zeus's children she decreed that they would not be born and sent the serpent Python to kill Leto. Leto managed to escape to the island of Delos which became the sacred birthplace of Apollo and Artemis. Another of Zeus's affairs which enraged Hera was with Semele, the daughter of Cadmus the King of Thebes. Hera appeared to Semele, disguised as an old neighbour of hers, and inquired about the mysterious lover she had taken. Hera suggested that she should ask him to appear in front of her in his true form. When Zeus next came to Semele she asked him who he was and when he refused to indulge his true identity she, in turn refused him entry to her bed. Just as Hera had planned, Zeus was outraged and consumed Semele with his thunderbolt. Semele was six months pregnant but Hermes rescued the child, a boy, and sowed it into the thigh of Zeus. Three months later the child sprang from the thigh of Zeus which is why he, Dionysus, was 'twice born' or 'the child of the double door.'

There was once an occasion of a rebellion against Zeus on Olympus when his behaviour had become just too intolerable for the others to bear. Hera, Poseidon, Apollo and the other Olympians, with the exception of Hestia, bound him with a rope tied with a 100 knots whilst he was asleep. Furiously he threatened them with death but, as his thunderbolt was out of reach, they just laughed at him. The Nereid Thetis foreseeing a civil war on Olympus fetched the Hundred Handed Briarus who, using all his hands at once, quickly untied him. Hera, as the perceived leader of the rebellion, bore the brunt of Zeus's revenge. He hung her up from the heavens bound by golden chains around her wrists and to make her discomfort worse he hung heavy anvils from her ankles. The rest of the deities were horrified by this punishment but were too afraid of Zeus to make much of a fuss. It was Zeus himself who relented in the end and freed Hera only after getting a firm assurance from everyone that they would not rebel again. Poseidon and Apollo were also singled out for special treatment as Zeus reckoned they had played a major role. They were sent to King Laomedon of Troy where they worked as virtual slaves for him and built the city walls. The rest of the gods were given a pardon on the aforementioned condition of towing the line in the future.

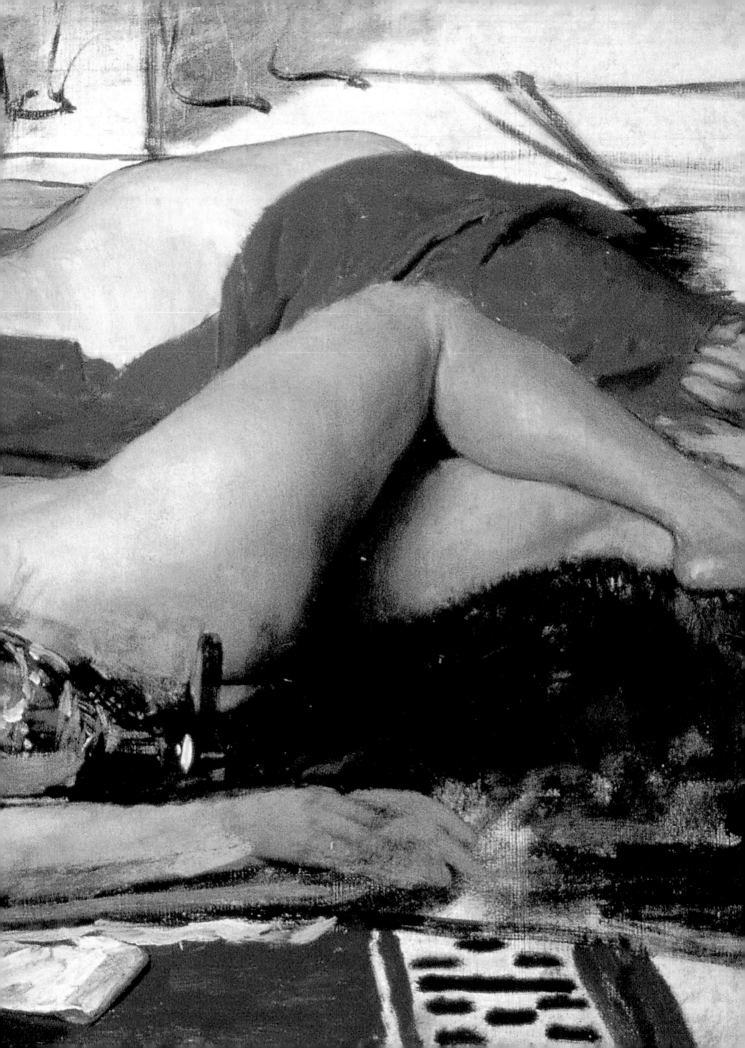

Chronological Table

MINOAN CIVILISATION

c3000 BC	Beginnings of Minoan civilisation in Crete
c2000 BC	Greek tribes spread into Greece itself
c1450 BC	Greek dynasty at Knossos
c1400 BC	Destruction of palace

MYCENEAN CIVILISATION

c1600 BC	Beginnings at Mycenae
c1300 BC	Highpoint of Mycenaean civilisation

c1200 BC	Widespread destruction of palaces
c1125 BC	Final destructrion of Mycenae

DARK AGES

1100-776 BC	Greek tribes migrate from mainland to Anatolia

GREEK CIVILISATION

776 BC	The first Olympiad and the starting point for Greek history
c750 BC	Greek colonisation of Italy begins
7th century	Sparta and Corinth major cities
490-480 BC	Persian wars
479-432 BC	Golden Age of Athens
431-404 BC	The Peloponnesian War Sparta defeats Athens
403-336 BC	Decline of city states. Power passes to Athens then Thebes then Philip of Macedonia takes all
336-300 BC	Alexander the Great leads the Greeks to conquest of known world
From 300 BC	The Hellenistic Age. Antigonids rule Greece Attalids rule Pergamum Seleucids rule from Antioch Ptolemies rule Egypt
146 AD	Greece becomes a province of Rome

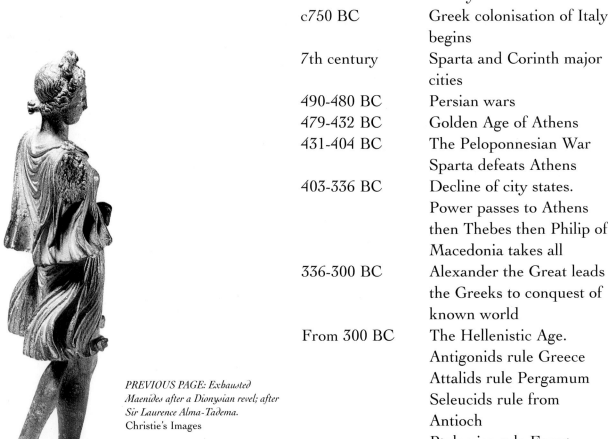

PREVIOUS PAGE: Exhausted Maenides after a Dionysian revel; after Sir Laurence Alma-Tadema.
Christie's Images

LEFT: Bronze statuette of Artemis.
Christie's Images